Soup & Ladle Favorites

100 Recipes from Pennsylvania Dietitians

Soup & Ladle Favorites

100 RECIPES FROM PENNSYLVANIA DIETITIANS

Pennsylvania Dietetic Association Foundation
(PADAF)
P.O. Box 60870
Harrisburg, Pennsylvania 17106-0870
717-233-0558

Edited, Designed, and Manufactured by
Favorite Recipes Press®, an imprint of

FRP

P. O. Box 305142
Nashville, Tennessee 37230
800-358-0560

Book Design: David Malone
Art Director: Steve Newman
Project Editor: Anne Lacy Boswell

Manufactured in the United States of America
First Printing: 2003
6,000 copies

Table of Contents

Preface 4

Acknowledgments 5

Soups 6 to 105

BEEF 6

PORK 16

POULTRY 32

SEAFOOD 50

VEGETABLE 60

LEGUME 94

FRUIT 104

Contributors 106

Common Measurements and Equivalents 107

Soup Glossary 108

Soup Tips 109

Index 110

Order Information 112

Preface

There's nothing like nutritious, delicious soup to warm the heart and bring cozy comfort to your family table. Soup can be served at anytime: as a first course, main dish, snack, or even dessert. Some soups are enough to make a complete meal. Anyone can make soup once you have an idea and the ingredients!

Dietitians from the Pennsylvania Dietetic Association know that first and foremost, good taste is the main reason we enjoy food. Because of this, we gathered 100 of our very best soup and stew recipes. It is our belief that all foods fit into a healthy diet and should be enjoyed in moderation.

The Pennsylvania Dietetic Association, a chapter of the American Dietetic Association, is the advocate of the dietetics profession serving the public through the promotion of optimal nutrition, health, and well-being. We are an organization of nearly 3,400 members throughout the Commonwealth of Pennsylvania. The Pennsylvania Dietetic Association Foundation's mission is to promote health through nutrition education and research for the public and the dietetic practitioner. The Foundation funds scholarships and awards education and research projects that promote optimal nutrition, health and well-being of the citizens of the Commonwealth of Pennsylvania. Profits from the sale of this cookbook will support our mission.

The recipe collection includes something for everyone—old family specialties, Pennsylvania classics, and contemporary "quickies" for hurried cooks. We hope you adopt a few new favorites of your own from us. ENJOY!

The Pennsylvania Dietetic Association Foundation

Acknowledgments

PENNSYLVANIA DIETETIC ASSOCIATION FOUNDATION BOARD

Manette Richardson, RD, CDE   President

Karen Virostek, MS, RD, FADA President-Elect

Rita Johnson, PhD, RD, FADA

Jeanne Lillis, MS, RD

Linda Pickwell, MS, RD

Barbara Williams, RD

MARKETING COMMITTEE

Denice Ferko-Adams, MPH, RD

Kathleen Dwyer, PhD, RD

Mary Klem, MS, RD, CNSD

Carol Landis, RD

COOKBOOK COORDINATOR

Jeanne Kandra, MS, RD

ADMINISTRATIVE SUPPORT

Colleen McCann, MPH, RD

PHOTOGRAPHY

Front Cover Photograph: SAN GIORGIO® Pasta

Back Cover Photograph: B. Foster Picture Perfect Productions

Meatball Soup

1 1/2 pounds extra-lean ground beef

1 egg, lightly beaten

1/2 cup plain bread crumbs

1 tablespoon dried parsley flakes

1/4 teaspoon salt

1 (14-ounce) can Italian-style diced tomatoes

1 (10-ounce) can beef broth

1 envelope onion soup mix

2 cups thinly sliced carrots

2 bay leaves

1/4 cup sliced celery tops

1/4 teaspoon pepper

1/4 teaspoon dried oregano leaves

1/4 teaspoon dried basil

RECIPE 1

Combine ground beef, egg, bread crumbs, parsley and salt in a bowl and mix well. Shape into 1-inch balls. Brown on all sides in a skillet; drain. Combine undrained tomatoes, broth, soup mix, carrots, bay leaves, celery, pepper, oregano and basil in a saucepan. Bring to a simmer and cook for 30 minutes or until carrots are tender. Add the meatballs and simmer for 30 minutes longer. Remove from heat and discard bay leaves. Ladle into bowls and sprinkle with grated Parmesan cheese. Serve with a green salad and crusty Italian bread. Yield: 6 servings.

Nutrients Per Serving: Calories 272; Protein 30 g; Carbohydrates 17 g; Total Fat 9 g; Saturated Fat 4 g; Cholesterol 81 mg; Fiber 2 g; Sodium 1004 mg

Meatball Stew en Casserole

1¹/2 pounds pearl onions, peeled

1¹/4 cups small carrots, halved lengthwise

1 (10-ounce) package frozen peas

2 pounds ground chuck

1 egg, lightly beaten

1 cup plain bread crumbs

2/3 cup milk

2¹/2 teaspoons salt

3/4 teaspoon each dried marjoram and Worcestershire sauce

1¹/2 pounds mushrooms

1 (10-ounce) can cream of mushroom soup

3/4 teaspoon seasoning and browning sauce

3/4 teaspoon each nutmeg and onion salt

2 pounds potatoes, cooked, mashed

1/4 cup milk

Steam onions and carrots, covered, in 1 inch of water in a large saucepan for 20 minutes or until tender-crisp; drain. Add peas; cover and set aside. Combine next 7 ingredients in a bowl and mix well. Shape into 1-inch balls. Brown on all sides in a skillet; drain, reserving the drippings. Sauté mushrooms in reserved drippings until tender; set aside. Combine next 4 ingredients in a saucepan and cook until heated through, stirring occasionally. Preheat oven to 375 degrees. Layer onions, carrots, peas, mushrooms and ground chuck in a 3-quart casserole dish. Pour mushroom soup mixture along the edges of the casserole. Spread mashed potatoes over the top; brush with milk. Bake for 60 minutes or until brown and bubbly. Yield: 10 servings.

Nutrients Per Serving: Calories 425; Protein 30 g; Carbohydrates 41 g; Total Fat 17 g; Saturated Fat 6 g; Cholesterol 89 mg; Fiber 6 g; Sodium 1135 mg

Hamburger Soup

2 tablespoons vegetable oil

2 large onions, sliced

1$\frac{1}{2}$ pounds ground beef

1 (28-ounce) can whole tomatoes

1 (14-ounce) can whole tomatoes

3 cups water

$\frac{1}{2}$ cup red wine

2 garlic cloves, minced

2 tablespoons sugar

1 envelope beefy onion soup mix

1 teaspoon dried basil

pepper to taste

1 pound carrots, sliced, cooked

RECIPE 3

Heat oil in a Dutch oven. Add onions and sauté until tender. Add ground beef and brown, stirring until crumbly; drain. Add undrained tomatoes, water, wine, garlic, sugar, soup mix, basil and pepper and mix well. Cook on low heat for 60 minutes or until ready to serve. Taste and adjust seasonings. Stir in carrots just before serving. Yield: 10 servings.

Nutrients Per Serving: Calories 247; Protein 17 g; Carbohydrates 16 g; Total Fat 13 g; Saturated Fat 4 g; Cholesterol 49 mg; Fiber 3 g; Sodium 295 mg

What's for Dinner Hamburger Soup

1 pound lean ground beef

2 ribs celery, chopped

2 (14-ounce) cans diced tomatoes

1 medium onion, chopped

1 garlic clove, minced

2 (10-ounce) cans beef broth

1 (16-ounce) package frozen broccoli, cauliflower and carrots

salt and pepper to taste

Brown ground beef in a saucepan, stirring until crumbly; drain. Add celery, undrained tomatoes, onion, garlic, broth, frozen vegetables, salt and pepper. Bring to a boil; reduce heat to low. Simmer, covered, for 60 minutes, stirring occasionally. Yield: 8 servings.

Nutrients Per Serving: Calories 174; Protein 15 g; Carbohydrates 10 g; Total Fat 8 g;
Saturated Fat 3 g; Cholesterol 41 mg; Fiber 3 g; Sodium 753 mg

Easy Minestrone

1 pound ground beef

2 small carrots, julienned

1 cup chopped celery

1/2 cup chopped onion

8 cups beef broth

1/2 teaspoon dried basil

1/2 teaspoon dried oregano leaves

1/4 teaspoon freshly ground pepper

6 ounces pastina, uncooked

1 (10-ounce) package frozen chopped spinach

1 (19-ounce) can chick-peas, drained

2 tablespoons grated Parmesan cheese

Brown ground beef in a saucepan over medium heat, stirring until crumbly; drain. Add carrots, celery and onion and sauté until tender. Add broth, basil, oregano and pepper. Bring to a boil; reduce heat. Simmer, covered, for 30 minutes, stirring occasionally. Stir in pastina and spinach and cook 10 minutes or until pasta is tender, stirring occasionally. Stir in chick-peas and cheese just before serving. Yield: 6 servings.

Nutrients Per Serving: Calories 433; Protein 31 g; Carbohydrates 47 g; Total Fat 13 g; Saturated Fat 5 g; Cholesterol 55 mg; Fiber 7 g; Sodium 1448 mg

Chili Meatball Supper

1 small yellow onion, chopped

1 small green bell pepper, chopped

1 (15-ounce) can kidney beans

1 (14-ounce) can stewed tomatoes

1 (8-ounce) can yellow corn

1 (8-ounce) can tomato sauce

1 cup beef broth

2 tablespoons sugar

2 teaspoons chili powder

1/4 teaspoon crumbled bay leaf

24 frozen meatballs

2 cups chopped cabbage

10 teaspoons low-fat shredded Cheddar cheese

Combine onion, green pepper, undrained beans, undrained tomatoes, undrained corn, tomato sauce, broth, sugar, chili powder and bay leaf in a large saucepan and mix well. Bring to a boil. Add meatballs and cabbage. Reduce heat; cover and simmer for 45 minutes, stirring occasionally. Ladle into bowls and sprinkle each serving with 1 teaspoon cheese. Yield: 10 (6-ounce) servings.

Nutrients Per Serving: Calories 197; Protein 9 g; Carbohydrates 21 g; Total Fat 10 g;
Saturated Fat 4 g; Cholesterol 12 mg; Fiber 4 g; Sodium 790 mg

Taco Orzo Soup

8 ounces lean ground beef

5 cups water

4 beef bouillon cubes

1 cup medium salsa

3/4 teaspoon chili powder

1/4 teaspoon cumin

6 ounces orzo, uncooked

Brown ground beef in a saucepan, stirring until crumbly; drain. Add water, bouillon cubes, salsa, chili powder and cumin; bring to a boil. Stir in orzo; reduce heat. Cook for 12 minutes or until orzo is tender, stirring frequently. Ladle into soup bowls and top with sliced green onions, crushed tortilla chips and sour cream. Yield: 7 (1-cup) servings.

Orzo is a tiny rice-shaped pasta that is a wonderful substitute for rice.

Nutrients Per Serving: Calories 175; Protein 11 g; Carbohydrates 21 g; Total Fat 5 g; Saturated Fat 2 g; Cholesterol 23 mg; Fiber 1 g; Sodium 678 mg

Quick Italian Beef and Vegetable Soup

1 pound lean ground beef

1 garlic clove, crushed

1 (14-ounce) can Italian-style stewed tomatoes

2 (14-ounce) cans beef broth

1 cup (1/4-inch-thick) sliced carrots

1/4 teaspoon salt

1/4 teaspoon pepper

1 (15-ounce) can Great Northern beans, drained, rinsed

1 medium zucchini, cut lengthwise in half and sliced 1/4-inch thick

2 cups chopped fresh spinach

Brown ground beef with garlic in a large saucepan, stirring until ground beef is crumbly; drain. Drain and chop tomatoes, reserving the liquid. Stir in tomatoes, reserved liquid, broth, carrots, salt and pepper. Bring to a boil. Reduce heat to low and simmer for 10 minutes. Stir in beans and zucchini and cook until zucchini is tender-crisp. Remove from heat and stir in spinach. Yield: 8 (1-cup) servings.

Nutrients Per Serving: Calories 226; Protein 20 g; Carbohydrates 17 g; Total Fat 9 g;
Saturated Fat 3 g; Cholesterol 41 mg; Fiber 4 g; Sodium 1049 mg

Italian Vegetable Soup with Beef

1 pound ground beef

2 (15-ounce) cans kidney beans, drained, rinsed

1 (15-ounce) can tomato sauce

1 (14-ounce) can diced tomatoes

2 cups (or more) water

1 cup chopped onion

1 cup chopped celery

1 cup chopped carrots

2 garlic cloves, minced

5 teaspoons beef bouillon granules

1 tablespoon dried parsley flakes

1/2 teaspoon dried oregano leaves

1/2 teaspoon dried basil

2 cups chopped cabbage

1 (15-ounce) can whole kernel corn

1 (15-ounce) can green beans

8 ounces macaroni, uncooked

Brown ground beef in a large saucepan, stirring until ground beef is crumbly; drain. Stir in kidney beans, tomato sauce, undrained tomatoes, water, onion, celery, carrots, garlic, bouillon, parsley, oregano and basil. Simmer over medium heat for 20 minutes. Stir in cabbage, undrained corn, undrained green beans and macaroni. Bring to a boil; reduce heat. Simmer until pasta is just tender. Add more water if needed. Yield: 8 servings.

Nutrients Per Serving: Calories 407; Protein 25 g; Carbohydrates 59 g; Total Fat 9 g; Saturated Fat 3 g; Cholesterol 41 mg; Fiber 9 g; Sodium 1534 mg

Wedding Soup

1 (3- to 4-pound) chicken, cut up

1 rib celery, coarsely chopped

1 carrot, coarsely chopped

salt and pepper to taste

2 pounds ground chuck

1 cup (4 ounces) grated Romano cheese

1 cup plain bread crumbs

1 egg, lightly beaten

1/4 teaspoon each salt, pepper and garlic salt

1/4 teaspoon dried parsley flakes

2 chicken bouillon cubes

2 heads endive, chopped

2 eggs

4 tablespoons grated Romano cheese

RECIPE 10

Combine chicken, celery, carrot, salt and pepper in a stockpot. Add enough water to cover and bring to a boil. Partially cover and reduce heat to a slow simmer. Cook just until the meat falls from the bone, about 1 1/2 to 2 hours. Strain, reserving the stock. Discard celery and carrot. Separate the chicken from the bones and tear into bite-size pieces. Return chicken and reserved stock to the saucepan. Combine ground chuck, cheese, bread crumbs, egg, 1/4 teaspoon salt, 1/4 teaspoon pepper, garlic salt and parsley in a bowl and mix well. Shape into 1-inch balls. Bring the stock to a boil. Add meatballs, bouillon cubes and endive. Reduce heat and simmer. Whisk eggs and cheese together in a small bowl. Pour into the soup, stirring continuously, until the eggs are cooked. Yield: 12 servings.

Nutrients Per Serving: Calories 392; Protein 40 g; Carbohydrates 13 g; Total Fat 20 g; Saturated Fat 8 g; Cholesterol 168 mg; Fiber 3 g; Sodium 646 mg

Creamy Ham and Potato Soup

1 tablespoon margarine

1 medium onion, finely chopped

5 potatoes, peeled, diced

1^1/2 cups water

1^1/2 cups low-fat milk

8 ounces lean cooked ham, cubed

^{1}/8 teaspoon white pepper

2 tablespoons cornstarch

Melt margarine in a large saucepan. Add onion and cook over low heat until tender. Add potatoes and water. Bring to a boil; reduce heat. Simmer, covered, for 15 minutes or until potatoes are soft. Stir in milk, ham and white pepper. Dissolve cornstarch in a small amount of water in a bowl. Stir into the soup. Cook over medium heat for 20 minutes, stirring occasionally. Yield: 6 (1-cup) servings.

Nutrients Per Serving: Calories 284; Protein 17 g; Carbohydrates 39 g; Total Fat 7 g; Saturated Fat 2 g; Cholesterol 40 mg; Fiber 3 g; Sodium 88 mg

Philadelphia Pepper Pot Soup

1 tablespoon margarine

1/2 cup 1/2-inch thick sliced celery

1/3 cup diced onion

1/4 cup diced ham

2 tablespoons finely diced leeks or green onions

6 cups water

5 chicken bouillon cubes

5 beef bouillon cubes

1 (14-ounce) can diced tomatoes

1 cup cooked rice

4 ounces tripe, cooked, julienned

1/2 cup diced green bell pepper

2 teaspoons salt

R E C I P E 12

Melt margarine in a large saucepan. Add celery, onion, ham and leeks and sauté until vegetables are tender. Add water and bouillon cubes. Bring to a boil; reduce heat. Add tomatoes, rice, tripe, bell pepper and salt. Simmer for 5 minutes or until heated through. Yield: 9 servings.

Nutrients Per Serving: Calories 78; Protein 5 g; Carbohydrates 9 g; Total Fat 2 g; Saturated Fat 1 g; Cholesterol 16 mg; Fiber 1 g; Sodium 1722 mg

Italian Bacon Cabbage Soup

1 tablespoon butter

1 tablespoon olive oil

1 onion, chopped

1 head cabbage, shredded

4 thick slices bacon

8 cups beef stock

3/4 cup rice

2 tablespoons chopped fresh parsley

salt and pepper to taste

1/2 cup grated Parmesan cheese

Heat butter and olive oil in a saucepan. Add onion and sauté until tender. Add cabbage and cook for 5 minutes, making sure the cabbage is well-coated with oil and butter. Fry bacon in a skillet until almost cooked through; drain and chop. Add bacon and beef stock to cabbage; bring to a boil; reduce heat. Simmer for 15 minutes. Stir in rice and return to a boil; reduce heat. Simmer for 15 to 20 minutes or until rice is tender, stirring occasionally. Stir in parsley, salt and pepper. Ladle into soup bowls and sprinkle with grated Parmesan cheese. Yield: 6 servings.

Nutrients Per Serving: Calories 274; Protein 10 g; Carbohydrates 37 g; Total Fat 10 g; Saturated Fat 4 g; Cholesterol 19 mg; Fiber 6 g; Sodium 1193 mg

Cauliflower Soup with Curried Onions

6 ounces thick-sliced bacon, cut into 1/4-inch cubes

2 cups sliced onions

1 1/2 teaspoons minced garlic

1/2 to 3/4 teaspoon curry powder

1/4 teaspoon cayenne pepper

1/2 teaspoon sugar

1 1/2 teaspoons flour

1 potato, peeled, coarsely chopped

1 3/4 teaspoons salt

1 head cauliflower, coarsely chopped

1 teaspoon turmeric

1/4 cup Major Grey's chutney

1/4 cup fresh parsley, minced

1 tablespoon fresh lemon juice

Fry bacon in a large skillet over medium heat until crisp; drain, reserving drippings. Sauté onions, garlic, curry powder and cayenne pepper in 2 1/2 tablespoons of the bacon drippings over high heat for 1 minute. Reduce heat to low. Cook, covered, until onions are tender, stirring occasionally. Add sugar. Cook over medium-high heat for 5 minutes or until onions are brown, stirring constantly. Stir in flour. Cook potato in 5 cups water and 1 teaspoon salt in covered saucepan for 10 minutes. Add cauliflower and turmeric. Cook, covered, for 10 minutes; cool for 10 minutes. Purée 3/4 of the cauliflower mixture with chutney in a food processor. Return to saucepan. Coarsely chop remaining cauliflower mixture in a food processor. Add to saucepan. Stir in onions. Simmer for 10 minutes. Stir in bacon, the remaining salt, parsley and lemon juice. Yield: 8 servings

Nutrients Per Serving: Calories 181; Protein 4 g; Carbohydrates 19 g; Total Fat 10 g; Saturated Fat 5 g; Cholesterol 13 mg; Fiber 3 g; Sodium 801 mg

B.L.T. Pasta Soup

4 ounces alphabet pasta, uncooked

2 (14-ounce) cans whole tomatoes

1 (14-ounce) can beef broth

1 cup water

salt and freshly ground pepper to taste

2 cups chopped iceberg lettuce

1 pound bacon, crisp-cooked, crumbled

Combine pasta, undrained tomatoes, broth and water in a medium saucepan. Bring to a boil. Boil for 5 minutes or until pasta is tender, stirring frequently. Season with salt and pepper. Place 1/3 cup of lettuce into each soup bowl. Ladle 1 cup of soup over lettuce. Sprinkle with bacon. Top with toasted croutons and a dollop of mayonnaise. Yield: 6 servings.

Nutrients Per Serving: Calories 251; Protein 13 g; Carbohydrates 20 g; Total Fat 14 g; Saturated Fat 4 g; Cholesterol 22 mg; Fiber 2 g; Sodium 1105 mg

Slow-Cooked Creamy Potato Soup

4 ounces Canadian bacon or 4 slices bacon

4 potatoes, cubed

1 onion, chopped

1 carrot, chopped

1 garlic clove, minced

1/2 cup uncooked pearl barley

1 bay leaf

thyme to taste

pepper to taste

2 (14-ounce) cans fat-free, reduced-sodium chicken broth

1/2 cup fat-free evaporated milk

1/4 cup fat-free half-and-half

Combine Canadian bacon, potatoes, onion, carrot, garlic, barley, bay leaf, thyme and pepper in a slow cooker. Pour in the broth and mix well. Cook, covered, on Low for 6 hours. Stir in the evaporated milk and half-and-half just before serving.
Yield: 6 (1 1/4-cup) servings.

Nutrients Per Serving: Calories 196; Protein 12 g; Carbohydrates 38 g; Total Fat 1 g;
Saturated Fat <1 g; Cholesterol 10 mg; Fiber 3 g; Sodium 290 mg

Philadelphia-Style Minestrone

RECIPE 17

1 (4-ounce) piece salt pork, diced

1 onion, sliced

1 garlic clove, minced

6 cups beef broth

4 tomatoes, diced

2 carrots, diced

2 ribs celery, diced

1 zucchini, sliced

1/4 head shredded cabbage

1 (19-ounce) can chick-peas, drained

1 (15-ounce) can kidney beans, drained

2 tablespoons vegetable oil

1 tablespoon dried parsley flakes

8 ounces macaroni, uncooked

salt and pepper to taste

Brown salt pork in a skillet. Add onion and garlic and sauté until tender. Place salt pork mixture in a slow cooker. Add broth, tomatoes, carrots, celery, zucchini, cabbage, chick peas, kidney beans, oil and parsley. Cook, covered, on Low for 6 hours. Add macaroni, salt and pepper. Cook, covered, on High for 30 minutes longer. Ladle into soup bowls and sprinkle with chopped fresh parsley and Parmesan cheese. Yield: 6 servings.

This South Philly Italian classic soup is made easy by cooking in a slow cooker.

Nutrients Per Serving: Calories 553; Protein 19 g; Carbohydrates 70 g; Total Fat 23 g; Saturated Fat 7 g; Cholesterol 16 mg; Fiber 11 g; Sodium 1604 mg

Bean and Sausage Soup

2 cups dried mixed beans

1 (28-ounce) can diced tomatoes

2 (14-ounce) cans chicken broth

2 cups frozen green peas, thawed

2 ribs celery, chopped

2 large carrots, chopped

1 red bell pepper, chopped

1 onion, chopped

1 cup white wine

1 1/2 pounds Italian sausage links, casings removed

RECIPE 18

Sort and rinse beans. Combine beans with enough water to cover by 2 inches in a saucepan. Bring to a boil and cook for 2 to 3 minutes. Cover and let stand in the refrigerator for 8 hours or overnight. Drain and rinse beans. Combine beans with undrained tomatoes, broth, peas, celery, carrots, bell pepper, onion and wine in a slow cooker. Cook, covered, on low for 7 to 8 hours. Cook sausage in a skillet over medium heat until cooked through. Slice 1/2 inch thick. Stir into the soup and cook 30 to 60 minutes longer. Yield: 8 servings.

Nutrients Per Serving: Calories 408; Protein 28 g; Carbohydrates 46 g; Total Fat 12 g; Saturated Fat 4 g; Cholesterol 35 mg; Fiber 16 g; Sodium 1214 mg

Kielbasa Stew

2 pounds kielbasa, cut into 1-inch slices

1¹/₂ pounds sauerkraut, drained, rinsed

2 Granny Smith apples, peeled, cored, sliced

1 onion, sliced into rings

2 pounds red potatoes, quartered

1¹/₂ cups chicken broth

¹/₂ teaspoon caraway seeds

¹/₂ cup (2 ounces) shredded Swiss cheese

Layer ¹/₂ of the kielbasa, the sauerkraut, remaining kielbasa, apples, onion and potatoes in a slow cooker. Pour in broth. Sprinkle with caraway seeds. Cook, covered, on high for 4 hours or until the potatoes are tender. Ladle into soup bowls and sprinkle each serving with 1 tablespoon cheese. Yield: 8 servings.

Nutrients Per Serving: Calories 312; Protein 13 g; Carbohydrates 31 g; Total Fat 17 g; Saturated Fat 7 g; Cholesterol 42 g; Fiber 6 g; Sodium 1247 mg

RECIPE 19

Reuben Soup

4 (14-ounce) cans chicken broth

1 pound kielbasa or Polish sausage,

halved lengthwise and cut into 1-inch slices

3 ounces medium egg noodles, uncooked

4 cups shredded cabbage

1/2 cup chopped onion

1 teaspoon caraway seeds

1/4 teaspoon garlic powder

1 cup (4 ounces) shredded Swiss cheese

RECIPE

Combine broth, kielbasa, noodles, cabbage, onion, caraway seeds and garlic powder in a saucepan. Bring to a boil; reduce heat. Simmer, covered, for 15 minutes or until cabbage and noodles are tender. Ladle into soup bowls and sprinkle each serving with cheese. Yield: 10 servings.

Nutrients Per Serving: Calories 209; Protein 4 g; Carbohydrates 10 g; Total Fat 12 g; Saturated Fat 5 g; Cholesterol 69 mg; Fiber 1 g; Sodium 1264 mg

Portuguese Soup

6 cups chicken broth

1 pound low-fat kielbasa, diced

1 pound boiling potatoes, peeled, diced

1 (15-ounce) can kidney beans, drained

1 (14-ounce) can diced tomatoes

1 medium onion, chopped

1 large carrot, diced

1/2 head cabbage, coarsely chopped

1/2 green bell pepper, diced

3 garlic cloves, minced

freshly ground pepper to taste

Combine broth, kielbasa, potatoes, kidney beans, undrained tomatoes, onion, carrot, cabbage, bell pepper and garlic in a large saucepan. Bring to a boil, stirring occasionally. Reduce heat and simmer for 2 hours or until thickened, stirring occasionally. Season with pepper. Yield: 12 servings.

Nutrients Per Serving: Calories 128; Protein 8 g; Carbohydrates 20 g; Total Fat 2 g; Saturated Fat <1 g; Cholesterol 8 mg; Fiber 4 g; Sodium 565 mg

Lentil Sausage Soup

2 cups dried lentils

8 ounces kielbasa, chopped

2 cups chopped onions

2 garlic cloves, minced

2 quarts water

1 (14-ounce) can diced tomatoes

2 cups sliced carrots

1 cup sliced celery

1 tablespoon chopped fresh rosemary

2 teaspoons salt

8 ounces egg noodles, cooked

RECIPE 22

Sort and rinse lentils. Sauté kielbasa, onions and garlic in a large saucepan until onions are tender. Add lentils, water, tomatoes, carrots, celery, rosemary and salt. Bring to a boil; reduce heat. Simmer, covered, for 50 minutes or until vegetables are tender. Spoon 1/3 cup noodles into each soup bowl; ladle soup over noodles. Sprinkle with chopped fresh parsley. Yield: 12 servings.

Nutrients Per Serving: Calories 224; Protein 12 g; Carbohydrates 37 g; Total Fat 4 g; Saturated Fat 1 g; Cholesterol 24 mg; Fiber 9 g; Sodium 548 mg

Clancy's Pub Soup

2 ribs celery, finely diced

2 medium carrots, finely diced

2 garlic cloves, minced

1 each onion and green bell pepper, finely diced

1 bay leaf

1 tablespoon dried basil

1 teaspoon pepper

$1/2$ teaspoon nutmeg

$1/4$ teaspoon dried thyme

12 ounces Railbender Ale

2 quarts chicken stock

5 ounces mild sausage links

$3/4$ cup diced cabbage

salt to taste

Tabasco sauce to taste

Sauté first 5 ingredients in a large saucepan sprayed with nonstick cooking spray until tender. Stir in bay leaf, basil, pepper, nutmeg and thyme. Add ale. Cook over high heat until mixture is reduced by $1/2$, stirring occasionally. Stir in stock, sausage and cabbage. Season with salt and Tabasco sauce. Bring to a boil; reduce heat. Simmer for 45 minutes or until cabbage is soft. Discard bay leaf. Serve with hot cooked rice, pasta or barley. Yield: 12 (1-cup) servings.

There is an annual Souper Bowl on Super Bowl Sunday in Erie. Area chefs submit their best soup and often share their recipes with the public. Each ticketholder gets one vote. In 2002 there were 34 entries!

Nutrients Per Serving: Calories 58; Protein 2 g; Carbohydrates 5 g; Total Fat 2 g; Saturated Fat 1 g; Cholesterol 6 mg; Fiber 1 g; Sodium 547 mg

Italian Sausage Soup

12 ounces Italian sausage, casings removed

8 ounces mushrooms, thinly sliced (about 3 cups)

1 cup chopped onion

2 garlic cloves, minced

1 (28-ounce) can whole tomatoes

$5^{1}/_{4}$ cups water

5 beef bouillon cubes

$1^{1}/_{2}$ cups hearty red wine (cabernet sauvignon)

1 teaspoon dried basil

$^{1}/_{4}$ teaspoon freshly ground pepper

6 ounces small pasta, uncooked (orzo, ditalini or tubetti)

2 cups sliced quartered zucchini

Brown sausage in a saucepan over medium heat, stirring until crumbly; drain. Add mushrooms, onion and garlic and sauté until onion is tender. Drain and chop tomatoes, reserving liquid. Add tomatoes, reserved liquid, water, bouillon cubes, wine, basil and pepper to sausage mixture and mix well. Bring to a boil; reduce heat. Simmer, covered, for 15 minutes, stirring occasionally. Return to a boil; stir in pasta. Reduce heat to medium-high and cook 7 minutes, stirring frequently. Add zucchini. Simmer 5 minutes longer or until the pasta is done. Remove from heat and let stand for 10 minutes before serving. Ladle into soup bowls and sprinkle with Parmesan cheese. Yield: 14 (1-cup) servings.

Nutrients Per Serving: Calories 127; Protein 6 g; Carbohydrates 15 g; Total Fat 4 g; Saturated Fat 1 g; Cholesterol 10 mg; Fiber 1 g; Sodium 510 mg

Italian Special Soup with Sausage

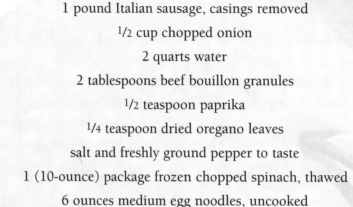

1 pound Italian sausage, casings removed

1/2 cup chopped onion

2 quarts water

2 tablespoons beef bouillon granules

1/2 teaspoon paprika

1/4 teaspoon dried oregano leaves

salt and freshly ground pepper to taste

1 (10-ounce) package frozen chopped spinach, thawed

6 ounces medium egg noodles, uncooked

Brown sausage with onion in a saucepan over medium heat, stirring until sausage is crumbly; drain. Stir in water, bouillon, paprika, oregano, salt and pepper and bring to a boil. Add spinach and noodles and mix well. Cook for 4 minutes or until noodles are tender. Yield: 6 servings.

Nutrients Per Serving: Calories 255; Protein 14 g; Carbohydrates 24 g; Total Fat 11 g; Saturated Fat 4 g; Cholesterol 57 mg; Fiber 2 g; Sodium 1261 mg

Pepperoni Pizza Soup

8 ounces Italian sausage, casings removed

1¼ cups sliced mushrooms

½ cup finely chopped onion

½ cup finely chopped green bell pepper

1 (15-ounce) can pizza sauce

2 cups water

1 cup chopped pepperoni

1 cup chopped plum tomatoes

¼ teaspoon Italian seasoning

¼ cup grated Parmesan cheese

RECIPE 26

Brown sausage in a saucepan over medium heat, stirring until crumbly; drain. Add mushrooms, onion and bell pepper and sauté until vegetables are tender. Stir in pizza sauce, water, pepperoni, tomatoes and Italian seasoning. Cover and bring to a boil; reduce heat. Simmer, covered, for 20 minutes, stirring occasionally. Stir in Parmesan cheese just before serving. Ladle into soup bowls and sprinkle with shredded mozzarella cheese. Serve with focaccia. Yield: 6 servings.

Nutrients Per Serving: Calories 244; Protein 12 g; Carbohydrates 11 g; Total Fat 17 g; Saturated Fat 7 g; Cholesterol 38 mg; Fiber 2 g; Sodium 1069 mg

Chicken Soup

1 onion, coarsely chopped

1 (3- to 4-pound) chicken, cut up

1 carrot, coarsely chopped

1 rib celery, coarsely chopped

2 sprigs fresh parsley

1 tablespoon salt, or to taste

pepper to taste

27

RECIPE

Sauté onion in a skillet sprayed with nonstick cooking spray until tender; set aside. Combine chicken with enough water to cover in a stockpot and bring to a boil; reduce heat. Simmer, partially covered, for 1 hour. Add onion, carrot, celery, parsley, salt and pepper. Cook just until the meat falls from the bone, about 30 to 60 minutes longer. Strain, pressing on the chicken and vegetables to extract as much juice as possible. Let stock cool to room temperature; refrigerate. Skim any solid fat from surface before reheating. Yield: 12 (1-cup) servings.

The addition of the chicken feet, gizzards, and heart makes a delicious rich stock. If you desire to retain the flavor of the chicken, add hot water to cover. For a full-flavored soup, cover with cold water.

Nutrients Per Serving: Calories 113; Protein 16 g; Carbohydrates 1 g; Total Fat 4 g; Saturated Fat 1 g; Cholesterol 48 mg; Fiber <1 g; Sodium 634 mg

Easy Chicken Noodle Soup

1 tablespoon butter

1/2 cup chopped onion

1/2 cup chopped celery

4 (14-ounce) cans chicken broth

1 (14-ounce) can vegetable broth

1 cup chopped cooked chicken

1 1/2 cups egg noodles, uncooked

1 cup sliced carrots

1/2 teaspoon dried basil

1/2 teaspoon dried oregano leaves

salt and pepper to taste

Melt butter in a large saucepan over medium heat. Add onion and celery and sauté until tender. Add chicken broth, vegetable broth, chicken, noodles, carrots, basil, oregano, salt and pepper; mix well. Bring to a boil; reduce heat. Simmer for 20 minutes or until heated through, stirring occasionally. Yield: 6 servings.

Nutrients Per Serving: Calories 259; Protein 19 g; Carbohydrates 28 g; Total Fat 7 g; Saturated Fat 3 g; Cholesterol 36 mg; Fiber 2 g; Sodium 1990 mg

Quick Chicken Noodle Soup

3 quarts water

5 chicken bouillon cubes

1 cup thinly sliced carrots

1/2 cup chopped celery

1/2 cup finely chopped onion

1 bay leaf

1 teaspoon salt

1/4 teaspoon freshly ground pepper

1/4 teaspoon poultry seasoning

3 cups chopped cooked chicken

6 ounces medium egg noodles, uncooked

Combine water, bouillon cubes, carrots, celery, onion, bay leaf, salt, pepper and poultry seasoning in a 6-quart saucepan. Bring to a boil. Stir in chicken and noodles and cook 8 minutes or until vegetables and noodles are tender, stirring occasionally. Discard bay leaf. Yield: 13 (1-cup) servings.

Nutrients Per Serving: Calories 115; Protein 10 g; Carbohydrates 11 g; Total Fat 3 g; Saturated Fat 1 g; Cholesterol 37 mg; Fiber 1 g; Sodium 656 mg

Chicken Noodle Soup

1 teaspoon vegetable oil

1/2 cup minced onion

1/2 cup diced carrots

1/2 cup sliced celery

1/2 teaspoon garlic powder

2 tablespoons cornstarch

1/4 teaspoon dried oregano flakes

3 cups reduced-sodium chicken broth

2 cups diced peeled potatoes

1/4 cup chopped cooked chicken

1/2 cup low-fat milk

4 ounces yolk-free noodles, uncooked

Heat oil in a large saucepan over medium heat. Add onion, carrots, celery and garlic powder and sauté until tender. Sprinkle cornstarch and oregano over vegetables; cook for 1 minute. Stir in broth and potatoes. Bring to a boil; reduce heat. Simmer, covered, for 20 minutes. Add chicken, milk and noodles. Cook, covered, for 10 minutes or until noodles are tender. Yield: 4 (1 1/2-cup) servings.

Nutrients Per Serving: Calories 259; Protein 12 g; Carbohydrates 45 g; Total Fat 4 g; Saturated Fat 1 g; Cholesterol 12 mg; Fiber 3 g; Sodium 132 mg

Last-Minute Cheddar Chicken and Noodles

1 tablespoon vegetable oil

12 ounces boneless skinless chicken breasts,
cut into 1-inch pieces

$^1/_2$ teaspoon garlic powder

1 (14-ounce) can chicken broth

6 ounces medium or wide egg noodles, uncooked

1 (16-ounce) package frozen mixed vegetables

2 cups (8 ounces) shredded Cheddar cheese

Heat oil in a 5-quart saucepan over medium heat. Sprinkle chicken with garlic powder. Sauté chicken in oil until cooked through. Stir in broth. Bring to a boil. Stir in noodles and vegetables. Return to a boil; reduce heat. Simmer, covered, 10 minutes or until noodles are tender, stirring every 2 minutes. Stir in cheese until melted.

Yield: 4 servings.

Nutrients Per Serving: Calories 628; Protein 44 g; Carbohydrates 47 g; Total Fat 30 g; Saturated Fat 14 g; Cholesterol 146 mg; Fiber 6 g; Sodium 1076 mg

Hearty Chicken or Turkey Tortellini Soup

2 to 3 quarts chicken or turkey broth

1 (19-ounce) package frozen tortellini

3 cups chopped cooked chicken or turkey

5 ounces fresh spinach, rinsed, julienned

2 medium tomatoes, peeled, cut into 1-inch cubes

2 to 3 tablespoons thinly sliced green onions or chives

1/4 teaspoon pepper

Bring broth to a boil in a large saucepan; reduce heat. Add tortellini and simmer for 8 minutes or until tender. Add chicken, spinach, tomatoes, green onions and pepper and cook until just heated through, stirring occasionally. Yield: 15 (1-cup) servings.

Nutrients Per Serving: Calories 170; Protein 15 g; Carbohydrates 18 g; Total Fat 4 g; Saturated Fat 1 g; Cholesterol 32 mg; Fiber 1 g; Sodium 741 mg

Lemon Egg Soup

4 cups chicken broth

1/4 cup uncooked rice

1/4 cup fresh lemon juice

3 eggs, at room temperature

salt and pepper to taste

Bring broth to a boil in a saucepan. Stir in rice and return to a boil; reduce heat. Simmer for 15 to 20 minutes or until rice is tender, stirring occasionally. Remove from heat. Beat lemon juice into the eggs in a bowl. Whisk 1/2 of the broth gradually into egg mixture. Pour egg mixture gradually back into remaining broth, whisking constantly. Cook over low heat for 5 minutes or until the soup is thickened, stirring constantly. Season with salt and pepper. Ladle into soup bowls and top with chopped green onions. Yield: 6 servings.

Freshly squeezed lemon juice works best in this easy-to-make classic soup.

Nutrients Per Serving: Calories 94; Protein 7 g; Carbohydrates 8 g; Total Fat 3 g; Saturated Fat 1 g; Cholesterol 106 mg; Fiber <1 g; Sodium 549 mg

RECIPE 33

Chicken and Spinach Soup

3 cups chopped cooked chicken

1/2 teaspoon cornstarch

1 1/2 teaspoons salt

dash of pepper

4 cups chicken broth

1 teaspoon fresh gingerroot, puréed

8 ounces spinach, rinsed, torn into bite-size pieces

1/8 teaspoon white pepper

Toss chicken, cornstarch, 1/2 teaspoon of the salt and the pepper in a bowl. Combine broth and gingerroot in a 3-quart saucepan and bring to a boil. Stir in chicken mixture; return to a boil. Add spinach, the remaining salt and white pepper. Bring to a boil; reduce heat. Simmer, covered, until the spinach is tender. Yield: 6 (1-cup) servings.

Nutrients Per Serving: Calories 152; Protein 22 g; Carbohydrates 2 g; Total Fat 6 g; Saturated Fat 2 g; Cholesterol 53 mg; Fiber 1 g; Sodium 1181 mg

Chicken Potpie

1 (3- to 4-pound) chicken, cut up

1$\frac{1}{2}$ teaspoons salt

2 cups flour

1 tablespoon shortening

2 eggs, lightly beaten

2 to 3 tablespoons water

$\frac{1}{2}$ cup chopped celery

$\frac{1}{4}$ cup diced onion

$\frac{1}{2}$ teaspoon pepper

2 tablespoons dried parsley

4 to 6 medium potatoes, sliced

Combine chicken and 1 teaspoon of salt in a stockpot. Add enough water to cover and bring to a boil; reduce heat. Simmer, partially covered, just until the meat falls from the bone, about 1$\frac{1}{2}$ to 2 hours. Strain chicken; set aside stock. Combine flour and remaining $\frac{1}{2}$ teaspoon salt in a bowl. Cut in shortening until crumbly. Add eggs and water, mixing until the mixture forms a ball, adding more water if necessary. Roll out dough as thin as possible on a lightly floured surface. Cut into 1-inch squares. Separate the chicken from the bones and tear into bite-size pieces; set aside. Discard the skin and bones. Return stock to stockpot. Stir in celery, onion, pepper and parsley. Bring to a boil; reduce heat. Add layers of potatoes and squares alternately into the broth until all ingredients are used. Cook 20 minutes or until potatoes and potpie squares are tender. Add chicken and cook until heated through. Yield: 6 servings.

Unlike chicken potpie from other regions of the United States, Pennsylvania Dutch potpie uses noodles instead of pastry crust.

Nutrients Per Serving: Calories 514; Protein 43 g; Carbohydrates 59 g; Total Fat 13 g; Saturated Fat 3 g; Cholesterol 167 mg; Fiber 5 g; Sodium 709 mg

Chicken Corn Soup
with Rivels

1 1/2 cups flour

1/2 teaspoon salt

1 egg, lightly beaten

2 quarts chicken broth

2 cups chopped cooked chicken

3 cups whole kernel corn

Mix flour and salt in a bowl. Add the egg. Stir with a fork or your hands until mixture forms small (1/4- to 1/2-inch) round dumplings. Bring broth to a boil in a saucepan; reduce heat. Add chicken and corn. Gradually add rivels, stirring constantly so that they do not stick together. Simmer for 5 to 10 minutes or until rivels are cooked through, stirring occasionally. Ladle into soup bowls and sprinkle with chopped fresh parsley. Yield: 10 servings.

This classic Pennsylvania Dutch soup has been a favorite for many generations. In central Pennsylvania it's commonly served at town carnivals, auctions, and other community organization fund-raisers.

Nutrients Per Serving: Calories 193; Protein 15 g; Carbohydrates 24 g; Total Fat 4 g; Saturated Fat 1 g; Cholesterol 42 mg; Fiber 2 g; Sodium 772 mg

Chicken Gumbo

1 teaspoon canola oil

1/4 cup flour

3 cups reduced-sodium chicken broth

1 1/2 pounds boneless skinless chicken breasts,
cut into 1-inch strips

4 garlic cloves, minced

2 green onions, chopped

1 potato, cubed

1 cup each chopped onion and chopped carrots

1/4 cup chopped celery

2 tablespoons grated carrot

2 teaspoons cayenne pepper

1 whole bay leaf

1/2 teaspoon dried thyme

1/2 teaspoon black pepper

1 cup sliced okra

Heat canola oil in a large saucepan over medium-low heat. Reduce heat to low. Stir in flour and cook until mixture turns golden brown, stirring constantly with a wire whisk. Add broth gradually and cook for 2 minutes, whisking constantly to remove all the lumps. Add chicken, garlic, green onions, potato, onion, chopped carrots, celery, grated carrot, cayenne pepper, bay leaf, thyme and black pepper and mix well. Bring to a boil; reduce heat. Simmer for 20 to 30 minutes. Add okra and simmer for 15 to 20 minutes longer. Discard bay leaf. Ladle over hot cooked rice in soup bowls. Yield: 8 (1-cup) servings.

Nutrients Per Serving: Calories 158; Protein 20 g; Carbohydrates 12 g; Total Fat 3 g; Saturated Fat 1 g; Cholesterol 48 mg; Fiber 2 g; Sodium 93 mg

Texas Tortilla Soup

2½ pounds chicken breasts

4 to 5 cups water

1 (14-ounce) can each beef broth and tomatoes

1 small onion, chopped

1 green bell pepper, chopped

1 (15-ounce) can whole kernel corn, drained

1 tablespoon chopped fresh cilantro

1 teaspoon chili powder

½ teaspoon cumin

salt and pepper to taste

1 ounce tortilla chips (about 20)

1½ cups (6 ounces) shredded Cheddar or Monterey Jack cheese

1 avocado, sliced

chopped fresh cilantro to taste

Combine chicken and water in a stockpot. Bring to a boil; reduce heat. Simmer, partially covered, just until the meat falls from the bone, about 45 minutes. Strain, reserving 4 cups of stock. Separate the chicken from the bones and tear into bite-size pieces; set aside. Discard the skin and bones. Return the reserved stock to the stockpot. Stir in beef broth, undrained tomatoes, onion and bell pepper and cook for 10 minutes over medium heat. Add chicken, corn, cilantro, chili powder, cumin, salt and pepper and mix well. Simmer for 10 minutes longer. Crush tortilla chips into 6 bowls. Ladle the soup over the chips and sprinkle each serving with ¼ cup cheese. Top with avocado slices and sprinkle with cilantro. Yield: 6 servings.

If you're in a hurry, use prepared chicken strips and 4 cups of reduced-sodium chicken broth.

Nutrients Per Serving: Calories 475; Protein 50 g; Carbohydrates 22 g; Total Fat 21 g; Saturated Fat 8 g; Cholesterol 135 mg; Fiber 5 g; Sodium 1057 mg

Hearty Chicken Taco Soup

3 cups chopped cooked chicken

2 (28-ounce) cans reduced-sodium

diced tomatoes

2 (15-ounce) cans black beans, drained, rinsed

2 (15-ounce) cans whole kernel corn,

drained, rinsed

1 envelope ranch dressing mix

1 envelope reduced-sodium taco seasoning mix

2 to 4 cups water or reduced-sodium

chicken broth

nonstick cooking spray

6 small flour tortillas

3/4 cup fat-free sour cream

1 1/2 cups (6 ounces) shredded Monterey Jack cheese

Combine chicken, undrained tomatoes, black beans, corn, ranch dressing mix and taco seasoning mix in a large saucepan. Bring to a simmer. Add 2 cups of water or more as needed. Simmer for 30 minutes. Spray baking sheet with nonstick cooking spray. Place tortillas on baking sheet and spray each tortilla with nonstick cooking spray. Bake at 350 degrees for 5 minutes or until slightly crisp. Cut into 1/4-inch-thick strips. Ladle soup into soup bowls. Top each serving with tortilla strips and 1 tablespoon of sour cream. Sprinkle with 2 tablespoons cheese. Yield: 12 servings.

Nutrients Per Serving: Calories 324; Protein 21 g; Carbohydrates 41 g; Total Fat 9 g; Saturated Fat 4 g; Cholesterol 39 mg; Fiber 8 g; Sodium 960 mg

Barley Turkey Chili

2 tablespoons margarine

1 pound ground turkey

3/4 cup chopped onion

1/2 chopped green bell pepper

3 cups water

1 (15-ounce) can red kidney beans

1 (6-ounce) can reduced-sodium tomato paste

1/2 cup uncooked pearl barley

1 tablespoon chili powder

1 tablespoon dried parsley flakes

2 teaspoons dry mustard

1 teaspoon cayenne pepper

1 teaspoon paprika

1/2 teaspoon garlic powder

3/4 cup (3 ounces) shredded low-fat Cheddar cheese

RECIPE 40

Melt margarine in a large saucepan. Add turkey, onion and bell pepper and cook until turkey is brown and crumbly, stirring constantly; drain. Add water, undrained kidney beans, tomato paste, barley, chili powder, parsley, mustard, cayenne pepper, paprika and garlic powder. Bring to a boil, stirring frequently; reduce heat. Simmer, covered, for 30 minutes, stirring occasionally. Uncover; simmer for 30 minutes longer, stirring occasionally. Ladle over hot cooked noodles or rice in soup bowls; sprinkle each serving with cheese. Yield: 10 (1-cup) servings.

Nutrients Per Serving: Calories 207; Protein 15 g; Carbohydrates 20 g; Total Fat 8 g;
Saturated Fat 2 g; Cholesterol 35 mg; Fiber 4 g; Sodium 285 mg

Turkey Chili

2 teaspoons canola oil

1/2 cup diced green bell pepper

1/2 cup diced onion

1/2 cup diced carrots

1/2 cup diced celery

1 to 1 1/2 pounds lean ground turkey

1 (15-ounce) can kidney beans or pinto beans,
drained, rinsed

1 (14-ounce) can no-salt added diced tomatoes

1 (6-ounce) can tomato paste

1 1/2 to 2 cups water

2 tablespoons chili powder

1/2 teaspoon garlic powder

1/2 teaspoon dried oregano leaves

1/2 teaspoon each cumin, paprika, salt and pepper

Coat a Dutch oven with nonstick cooking spray. Add canola oil and heat over medium heat. Add bell pepper, onion, carrots and celery and sauté until tender. Add turkey and cook until brown and crumbly, stirring constantly. Stir in beans, undrained tomatoes, tomato paste, water, chili powder, garlic powder, oregano, cumin, paprika, salt and pepper. Simmer for 30 minutes. Ladle into soup bowls and top with sour cream, shredded Cheddar cheese, chopped green onions or sliced black olives. Yield: 10 (1-cup) servings.

Nutrients Per Serving: Calories 154; Protein 16 g; Carbohydrates 14 g; Total Fat 4 g; Saturated Fat <1 g; Cholesterol 28 mg; Fiber 4 g; Sodium 486 mg

White Lightning Chili with Turkey

2 cups dried navy beans, sorted, rinsed

4 (14-ounce) cans reduced-sodium chicken broth

1 large onion, chopped

2 garlic cloves, minced

1 tablespoon white pepper

1 tablespoon each dried oregano leaves and cumin

1/2 teaspoon ground cloves

5 cups chopped cooked turkey

16 ounces kielbasa, sliced

1 cup water

2 (4-ounce) cans chopped green chiles, drained

1 jalapeño chile, seeded, chopped

1 teaspoon salt

Combine beans with enough water to cover by 2 inches in a bowl. Let soak 8 hours; drain. Combine beans, 3 cans of the broth, onion, garlic, white pepper, oregano, cumin and cloves in a Dutch oven and mix well. Bring to a boil; reduce heat. Simmer, covered, for 2 hours or until beans are tender, stirring occasionally. Stir in remaining broth, turkey, kielbasa, water, green chiles, jalapeño chile and salt. Bring to a boil; reduce heat. Simmer, covered, for 1 hour, stirring occasionally. Ladle into soup bowls and top with shredded Cheddar cheese, salsa, sour cream or green onions. Yield: 8 servings.

The "lightning" comes from the jalapeño chile. The seeds of the chile are extremely hot, so be sure to remove all of them unless you want your chili really spicy! You may substitute 16 ounces of andouille, a Cajun-style sausage, for the kielbasa or prepare the chili without sausage.

Nutrients Per Serving: Calories 460; Protein 45 g; Carbohydrates 38 g; Total Fat 14 g; Saturated Fat 5 g; Cholesterol 88 mg; Fiber 14 g; Sodium 1094 mg

Cabbage Soup

2 onions, chopped

2 pounds lean ground turkey or beef

4 to 8 bouillon cubes

1 head cabbage, chopped

6 cups water

1 (28-ounce) can crushed tomatoes

1 (11-ounce) can tomato soup

$1/2$ teaspoon pepper

1 to 2 cups cooked rice

Sauté onions in a large saucepan sprayed with nonstick cooking spray until tender. Add ground turkey and cook, stirring until brown and crumbly; drain. Add bouillon cubes and cabbage and cook over medium heat until cabbage is tender. Add water, undrained tomatoes, soup and pepper and mix well. Simmer for 2 to 3 hours. Add rice and cook until heated through. Yield: 10 servings.

Nutrients Per Serving: Calories 227; Protein 21 g; Carbohydrates 26 g; Total Fat 5 g; Saturated Fat <1 g; Cholesterol 37 mg; Fiber 4 g; Sodium 1277 mg

Skillet Goulash with Turkey

1 pound lean ground turkey

1/2 cup chopped yellow onion

1/2 cup chopped green bell pepper

1 (14-ounce) can diced tomatoes

1 cup reduced-sodium tomato sauce

6 ounces egg noodles, uncooked

1/2 cup chopped celery

1/2 cup (or more) water

2 teaspoons garlic powder

1 teaspoon onion powder

1 teaspoon sugar

3/4 teaspoon salt

1/4 teaspoon pepper

1/8 teaspoon dried basil

1/8 teaspoon dried marjoram

RECIPE 44

Brown ground turkey with onion and bell pepper in a skillet, stirring until ground turkey is crumbly; drain. Stir in undrained tomatoes, tomato sauce, noodles, celery, water, garlic powder, onion powder, sugar, salt, pepper, basil and marjoram. Bring to a boil; reduce heat. Simmer, covered, until noodles are tender, stirring occasionally. Add more water if needed. Yield: 7 (6-ounce) servings.

Nutrients Per Serving: Calories 187; Protein 16 g; Carbohydrates 23 g; Total Fat 4 g;
Saturated Fat <1 g; Cholesterol 49 mg; Fiber 2 g; Sodium 380 mg

Crab Tomato Soup

1/4 cup (1/2 stick) butter

1/4 cup finely chopped onion

1 garlic clove, minced

1/4 cup flour

1/2 teaspoon salt

1/8 teaspoon pepper

2 1/2 cups half-and-half

2 cups tomato juice

1/4 teaspoon Worcestershire sauce

1/4 teaspoon dried savory

dash hot red pepper sauce

2 (6-ounce) cans lump crab meat, rinsed,
drained, flaked

Melt butter in a 2-quart saucepan. Add onion and garlic and sauté until onion is tender. Stir in flour, salt and pepper and cook until bubbly. Gradually add half-and-half, tomato juice, Worcestershire sauce, savory and hot red pepper sauce. Bring to a boil, stirring constantly. Add crab meat and cook until heated through. Ladle into soup bowls and top with a dollop of sour cream. Sprinkle with parsley. Yield: 4 servings.

Nutrients Per Serving: Calories 413; Protein 19 g; Carbohydrates 19 g; Total Fat 30 g; Saturated Fat 18 g; Cholesterol 142 mg; Fiber 1 g; Sodium 1120 mg

Callaloo
(Crab and Greens Soup)

8 ounces callaloo greens

3 tablespoons butter

1/2 cup finely chopped onion

1/2 teaspoon minced garlic

3 cups chicken stock

1/2 cup coconut milk

1 teaspoon salt

freshly ground pepper to taste

1 cup crab meat

dash A-1 steak sauce

Rinse callaloo under cold running water, discarding the outer leaves. If using spinach or Swiss chard, rinse and cut into thin strips. Melt butter in a large saucepan until melted. Add onion and garlic and sauté until tender. Add callaloo until heated through and slightly wilted, stirring constantly. Add stock, coconut milk, salt and pepper and mix well. Bring to a boil; reduce heat to low. Simmer for 10 minutes or until greens are tender, stirring occasionally. Add crab meat and A-1 sauce and cook until crab meat is heated through, stirring frequently. Yield: 4 servings.

Callaloo, also known as dasheen or Chinese spinach, are the green leaves from the taro root, a Jamaican tuber. The leaves taste like a cross between broccoli and spinach. Use fresh spinach or Swiss chard as a substitute if you are unable to find callaloo.

Nutrients Per Serving: Calories 142; Protein 7 g; Carbohydrates 5 g; Total Fat 11 g; Saturated Fat 6 g; Cholesterol 46 mg; Fiber 1 g; Sodium 1285 mg

Shrimp and Sweet Potato Soup

3/4 cup diced yellow onion

1/3 cup each diced celery, red bell pepper and green bell pepper

1 tablespoon diced seeded jalapeño chile

1 tablespoon minced garlic

1 tablespoon each fresh thyme and marjoram, minced

1/4 teaspoon ground cloves

2 1/2 tablespoons olive oil

1 1/2 pounds sweet potatoes, cut into 1-inch cubes

6 cups shrimp stock, fish stock or clam juice

3 cups diced tomatoes

1 bay leaf

1 1/2 cups frozen whole kernel corn, thawed

3 tablespoons chopped fresh cilantro

1/3 cup sliced green onions

15 ounces cooked shrimp

Sauté the first 9 ingredients in olive oil in a large saucepan until vegetables are tender. Add sweet potatoes, stock, tomatoes, and bay leaf and mix well. Cover and bring to a boil. Reduce heat to low and simmer for 30 minutes or until sweet potatoes are tender. Stir in corn, cilantro and green onions. Cook until heated through, stirring occasionally. Stir in shrimp. Remove bay leaf. Ladle into soup bowls and accompany each serving with a lime wedge. Yield: 12 (6-ounce) servings.

Dried herbs can be substituted for fresh, but reduce the amount by one-third. You may use either cooked or raw shrimp. If using raw, cook the soup for 2 to 3 minutes longer after adding the shrimp or until the shrimp turn pink.

Nutrients Per Serving: Calories 174; Protein 12 g; Carbohydrates 23 g; Total Fat 5 g; Saturated Fat 1 g; Cholesterol 70 mg; Fiber 3 g; Sodium 293 mg

Manhattan Clam Chowder

2 (6-ounce) cans minced clams

1½ cups water

1 (14-ounce) can diced tomatoes

1 cup chopped onion

2 potatoes, peeled, chopped

½ cup finely chopped carrots

1 teaspoon salt

½ teaspoon dried thyme

freshly ground pepper to taste

Drain clams, reserving liquid. Add enough water to reserved liquid to measure 3 cups. Combine clam juice and water mixture, undrained tomatoes, onion, potatoes, carrots, salt, thyme and pepper in a large saucepan and mix well. Cook, covered, over medium heat for 30 to 35 minutes. Remove from heat. Mash vegetables slightly to thicken the broth. Stir in clams and return to heat. Cook until heated through, stirring occasionally. Yield: 6 servings.

Nutrients Per Serving: Calories 131; Protein 10 g; Carbohydrates 21 g; Total Fat 1 g;
Saturated Fat <1 g; Cholesterol 20 mg; Fiber 3 g; Sodium 504 mg

New England Clam Chowder

4 (6-ounce) cans minced clams

4 to 6 potatoes, peeled, chopped

1/2 cup chopped onion

2 1/2 cups milk

1 cup light cream

3 tablespoons flour

1/2 teaspoon Worcestershire sauce

3/4 teaspoon salt

pepper to taste

2 slices bacon, crisp-cooked, crumbled

Drain clams, reserving the liquid. Add enough water to reserved liquid to measure 2 cups. Combine clam juice and water mixture, potatoes and onion in a large saucepan. Cook, covered, over medium heat for 15 minutes or until potatoes are tender. Stir in clams, 2 cups of the milk and the cream. Combine remaining 1/2 cup milk with the flour in a small bowl and stir until smooth. Stir flour mixture into the chowder. Bring to a simmer, stirring frequently. Add Worcestershire sauce, salt and pepper and mix well. Ladle into bowls and sprinkle bacon on top. Yield: 6 servings.

Nutrients Per Serving: Calories 469; Protein 25 g; Carbohydrates 52 g; Total Fat 18 g; Saturated Fat 10 g; Cholesterol 100 mg; Fiber 4 g; Sodium 587 mg

Seafood Chowder

1 garlic clove, minced

1/2 cup chopped onion

3/4 cup chopped green or red bell pepper

3/4 cup sliced carrots

3/4 cup chopped potato

1 (28-ounce) can diced tomatoes

1 cup vegetable or chicken broth

2 teaspoons chili powder, or to taste

3/4 teaspoon cumin

1/4 teaspoon dried oregano leaves

1/2 teaspoon sugar

6 ounces cod or snapper, cubed

6 ounces deveined peeled fresh shrimp

water, as needed

pepper to taste

Sauté garlic, onion and bell pepper in a medium stockpot sprayed with nonstick cooking spray until tender. Add carrots, potato, undrained tomatoes, broth, chili powder, cumin, oregano and sugar and mix well. Simmer, covered, for 10 minutes. Stir in cod and shrimp. Cook for 10 minutes longer, or until fish is cooked through and shrimp is pink, adding water as needed. Stir in pepper. Yield: 4 servings.

Nutrients Per Serving: Calories 151; Protein 15 g; Carbohydrates 23 g; Total Fat 1 g; Saturated Fat <1 g; Cholesterol 72 mg; Fiber 6 g; Sodium 611 mg

Seafood Corn Chowder

1 tablespoon margarine

1 cup chopped onion

1/2 cup chopped green bell pepper

1/2 cup chopped red bell pepper

1/3 cup chopped celery

1 tablespoon flour

1 (10-ounce) can reduced-sodium chicken broth

2 cups skim milk

1 (12-ounce) can evaporated skim milk

8 to 12 ounces imitation crab meat, cubed

2 cups fresh or frozen whole kernel corn

1/2 teaspoon pepper

1/2 teaspoon paprika

Heat margarine in a large saucepan until melted. Add onion, bell peppers and celery and sauté until tender. Stir in flour. Cook for 2 minutes longer, stirring constantly. Gradually add broth. Bring to a boil; reduce heat to medium. Stir in milk, evaporated milk, crab meat, corn, pepper and paprika. Cook 5 minutes or until chowder is heated through, stirring occasionally. Yield: 6 servings.

You'll never miss the cream in this tasty chowder that is lower in fat from using skim milk.

Nutrients Per Serving: Calories 230; Protein 18 g; Carbohydrates 33 g; Total Fat 4 g; Saturated Fat 1 g; Cholesterol 33 mg; Fiber 2 g; Sodium 206 mg

Lobster Chowder

2 tablespoons butter or margarine

1/2 cup chopped celery

1/4 cup chopped onion

1 1/2 cups water

1 (16-ounce) package frozen mixed vegetables

1 bay leaf

1 (4-ounce) can sliced mushrooms

1 tablespoon cornstarch

1 cup tomato sauce

2 cups milk

1 cup canned lobster

RECIPE 52

Heat butter in a large saucepan until melted. Add celery and onion. Sauté until tender. Reduce heat to medium and add water, mixed vegetables and bay leaf. Cook, covered, for 10 minutes. Reduce heat to low and simmer for 5 minutes. Drain mushrooms, reserving the liquid. Combine cornstarch with reserved mushroom liquid in a small bowl and stir until smooth. Add cornstarch mixture to chowder, stirring constantly until thickened. Add mushrooms, tomato sauce, milk and lobster and mix well. Cook until heated through, being careful not to boil. Yield: 4 servings.

Nutrients Per Serving: Calories 279; Protein 18 g; Carbohydrates 31 g; Total Fat 11 g; Saturated Fat 6 g; Cholesterol 63 mg; Fiber 7 g; Sodium 838 mg

Fish Chowder
(A Real Maine Chowder)

4 large potatoes, cubed

4 slices of salt pork

1 large onion, chopped

2 pounds cod fillets

1 (12-ounce) can evaporated milk

4 cups milk

1/2 cup (1 stick) butter or margarine

salt and pepper to taste

Combine potatoes with enough water to cover in a saucepan. Bring to a boil; reduce heat. Simmer, covered, until potatoes are soft. Drain, reserving 1/2 cup of the cooking liquid. Fry salt pork in a saucepan until almost cooked through; discard salt pork. Sauté onion in the same saucepan until tender. Add potatoes and reserved cooking liquid to onion mixture. Remove from heat and set aside. Combine cod with enough water to cover in a saucepan. Simmer for 10 minutes or until it flakes easily; drain. Add cod, evaporated milk, milk, butter, salt and pepper to onion mixture. Cook over low heat until heated through, stirring frequently. Yield: 6 servings.

Nutrients Per Serving: Calories 615; Protein 31 g; Carbohydrates 37 g; Total Fat 40 g; Saturated Fat 21 g; Cholesterol 138 mg; Fiber 3 g; Sodium 591 mg

Smoked Trout Chowder

1 medium onion, diced

4 to 5 small red potatoes, cut into 1/2-inch cubes

1 tablespoon dried thyme

1 cup hot water

16 ounces clam juice

1 to 2 pounds smoked trout or

other white fish, flaked

1 cup fresh or frozen whole kernel corn

2 cups heavy cream

salt and pepper to taste

RECIPE 54

Sauté onion in a large saucepan sprayed with nonstick cooking spray until tender. Add potatoes and thyme and cook until heated through. Add hot water and clam juice. Bring to a boil; reduce heat. Simmer, covered, for 15 minutes or until potatoes are soft. Stir in trout, corn, heavy cream, salt and pepper. Simmer just until heated through, stirring occasionally. Yield: 6 servings.

Nutrients Per Serving: Calories 670; Protein 47 g; Carbohydrates 29 g; Total Fat 41 g; Saturated Fat 21 g; Cholesterol 231 mg; Fiber 3 g; Sodium 3227 mg

Cream of Asparagus Soup

1½ pounds fresh asparagus, trimmed

6 tablespoons (¾ stick) butter

1½ cups chopped onions

6 tablespoons flour

pinch of salt

2 cups water or reduced-sodium chicken broth

4 cups hot milk

2 tablespoons tamari or soy sauce

1 teaspoon dried dill weed

1 teaspoon salt

½ teaspoon white pepper

¾ cup boiling water

Coarsely chop asparagus stems. Set tips aside. Heat butter in a large saucepan until melted. Add asparagus stems and onions and sauté until onions are tender. Reduce heat to low. Add flour and pinch of salt and cook for 5 to 8 minutes, stirring constantly. Add water gradually and cook until thickened, stirring constantly. Process soup in a blender in batches, adding milk gradually, until puréed. Return soup to the saucepan. Stir in tamari, dill weed, 1 teaspoon salt and white pepper. Cook over medium-low heat for 10 minutes longer or until thickened; do not boil. Place asparagus tips in a skillet. Add water. Simmer, covered, until tender-crisp, about 2 minutes; drain. Add to soup and mix well. Cook just until heated through, stirring frequently. Yield: 6 servings.

Nutrients Per Serving: Calories 279; Protein 10 g; Carbohydrates 22 g; Total Fat 17 g; Saturated Fat 11 g; Cholesterol 53 mg; Fiber 3 g; Sodium 1024 mg

Creamed Beet Soup

4 quarts water

1/2 cup (1 stick) butter

1 small onion, thinly sliced

5 allspice berries

2 tablespoons white vinegar

1 large bay leaf

1 teaspoon salt

4 medium fresh beets, peeled, sliced

2 tablespoons flour

1/2 cup (or more) sour cream

Combine water, butter, onion, allspice, vinegar, bay leaf and salt in a large saucepan and bring to a boil. Add beets and cook until tender. Combine flour with 2 tablespoons of the beet liquid in a small bowl and stir to form a paste. Add sour cream and stir until smooth. Add flour mixture to the soup; cook until thickened, stirring constantly. Do not boil. Discard bay leaf. Process soup in a blender until puréed. Return soup to the saucepan. Bring to a simmer and cook until heated through, stirring frequently.

Yield: 10 servings.

Nutrients Per Serving: Calories 138; Protein 1 g; Carbohydrates 8 g; Total Fat 12 g;
Saturated Fat 7 g; Cholesterol 30 mg; Fiber <1 g; Sodium 359 mg

Creamy Broccoli Soup

1 tablespoon butter or margarine

1 small onion, thinly sliced

1 rib celery, sliced

$1/2$ cup water

$2^{1/2}$ cups chicken broth

2 tablespoons uncooked rice

1 teaspoon salt

2 cups cooked broccoli

$1/2$ cup evaporated milk

Melt butter in a large saucepan. Add onion and celery and cook over low heat until tender. Add water and simmer for 2 minutes. Stir in 1 cup of the broth, the rice and salt; bring to a boil. Reduce heat; simmer, covered, for 15 minutes or until rice is tender, stirring occasionally. Pour soup into a blender. Process until puréed. Return soup to saucepan and cook on medium-low heat. Pour remaining $1^{1/2}$ cups broth and the broccoli into the blender. Process until puréed. Add broccoli mixture and evaporated milk to the saucepan and mix well. Bring to a simmer and cook until heated through, stirring frequently. Yield: 6 servings.

Nutrients Per Serving: Calories 94; Protein 5 g; Carbohydrates 9 g; Total Fat 4 g; Saturated Fat 2 g; Cholesterol 12 mg; Fiber 2 g; Sodium 770 mg

Creamy Carrot Soup

2 teaspoons olive oil

1 pound carrots, chopped

1 medium onion, chopped

1 garlic clove, minced

4 cups chicken or vegetable broth

1 potato, peeled, diced

1 bay leaf

salt and pepper to taste

Heat olive oil in a large saucepan. Add carrots, onion and garlic and sauté until tender. Reduce heat to low; simmer, covered, for 10 minutes, stirring occasionally. Add broth, potato and bay leaf. Simmer, covered, for 30 minutes or until potato is soft. Discard bay leaf. Purée soup in batches in a blender until smooth. Return to stockpot. Season with salt and pepper and heat to serving temperature, stirring frequently. Ladle into soup bowls and top with a dollop of plain yogurt or sour cream and sprinkle with chopped fresh parsley or mint. Yield: 4 servings.

Nutrients Per Serving: Calories 161; Protein 8 g; Carbohydrates 25 g; Total Fat 4 g; Saturated Fat 1 g; Cholesterol 0 mg; Fiber 5 g; Sodium 820 mg

Carrot and Sweet Potato Soup

2 tablespoons peanut oil

1/4 cup coarsely chopped onion

1 tablespoon minced garlic

3/4 cup chopped carrots

1/2 cup dry white wine

2 medium sweet potatoes, peeled, coarsely chopped

1 dried ancho chile, seeded

1/2 tablespoon cumin

2 cups chicken broth

1/2 cup milk

salt and pepper to taste

Heat peanut oil in a large saucepan over medium heat. Add onion and sauté for 6 to 8 minutes or until tender. Add garlic, carrots and white wine. Reduce heat and simmer for 5 minutes. Add sweet potatoes, ancho chile, cumin and chicken broth and simmer for 30 to 40 minutes or until vegetables are tender. Strain soup, reserving liquid. Purée cooked vegetables in a blender or food processor while gradually adding reserved liquid. Return to saucepan. Add milk, salt and pepper and cook just until heated through, stirring frequently. Ladle into soup bowls and top with sour cream, guacamole or chopped fresh chives. Yield: 4 servings.

Nutrients Per Serving: Calories 219; Protein 6 g; Carbohydrates 26 g; Total Fat 9 g; Saturated Fat 2 g; Cholesterol 4 mg; Fiber 4 g; Sodium 439 mg

Corn Chowder

2 medium potatoes

2 tablespoons butter or margarine

1 medium onion, finely chopped

1 green bell pepper, chopped

1 tablespoon flour

2 (8-ounce) cans sweet corn, drained

1¼ cups milk

1 cup vegetable stock

1½ cups mushrooms, sliced

1 cup heavy cream

1 teaspoon salt

½ teaspoon white pepper

RECIPE 60

Combine potatoes with enough water to cover in a saucepan. Bring to a boil. Cook, covered, for 10 minutes; drain and cool. Finely chop potatoes and set aside. Melt butter in a skillet. Add onion and bell pepper and sauté until tender. Remove from heat. Stir in flour, using a wooden spoon, to make a paste; set aside. Combine potatoes, corn, milk and stock in a saucepan and bring to a boil over medium heat, stirring occasionally. Add 2 tablespoons of the liquid to the flour mixture. Stir to make a smooth, thick liquid. Stir into potato mixture. Add mushrooms and mix well. Reduce heat to low; cover and simmer for 15 to 20 minutes. Add cream, salt and white pepper and mix well. Cook until heated through. Yield: 4 servings.

Nutrients Per Serving: Calories 450; Protein 9 g; Carbohydrates 41 g; Total Fat 31 g; Saturated Fat 19 g; Cholesterol 107 mg; Fiber 5 g; Sodium 1103 mg

Gazpacho

2 plum tomatoes, seeded, quartered

1 green bell pepper, quartered

1 cucumber, peeled, halved

1 onion, halved

3 garlic cloves

1 (4-ounce) jar diced pimentos, drained

2 (12-ounce) cans tomato juice

$1/3$ cup red wine vinegar

$1/4$ cup olive oil

$1^1/2$ teaspoons salt

$1/4$ teaspoon hot red pepper sauce

$1/8$ teaspoon freshly ground pepper

1 (5-ounce) package seasoned croutons

Combine 1 tomato, $1/2$ of the bell pepper, $1/2$ of the cucumber, $1/2$ of the onion, 1 garlic clove, pimentos and $1/2$ cup of the tomato juice in a food processor or blender. Process until smooth. Pour into a large bowl. Stir in the remaining tomato juice, vinegar, olive oil, salt, hot red pepper sauce and pepper. Chill, covered, for 2 hours or until completely chilled. Chop the remaining tomato, bell pepper, cucumber and onion and mince the garlic; set aside. Ladle the soup into 6 chilled bowls and top each serving with the chopped vegetables, croutons and chopped fresh chives. Yield: 6 servings.

Nutrients Per Serving: Calories 241; Protein 4 g; Carbohydrates 27 g; Total Fat 14 g; Saturated Fat 3 g; Cholesterol 2 mg; Fiber 3 g; Sodium 1290 mg

RECIPE 61

Hot-and-Sour Soup

10 dried shiitake mushrooms

1 1/2 cups boiling water

3 (10-ounce) cans reduced-sodium chicken broth

8 ounces firm tofu, cut into 1/2-inch strips

3 tablespoons white wine vinegar

3 tablespoons reduced-sodium soy sauce

2 tablespoons cornstarch

2 teaspoons fish sauce

1/2 teaspoon crushed red pepper

1/4 teaspoon black pepper

1/4 cup minced green onion tops

1 teaspoon dark sesame oil

Combine mushrooms and boiling water in a bowl; cover and let stand for 15 minutes. Drain, reserving 1 cup of liquid. Discard stems; rinse and cut caps into thin strips. Combine 1/2 cup of the reserved mushroom liquid and broth in a large saucepan; bring to a boil. Add mushrooms and tofu. Reduce heat and simmer for 3 minutes. Combine the remaining 1/2 cup reserved mushroom liquid, the vinegar, soy sauce, cornstarch, fish sauce, red pepper and black pepper in a small bowl; stir until smooth. Add cornstarch mixture to the soup; bring to a boil. Cook 1 minute, stirring constantly. Remove from heat; stir in green onions and sesame oil. Yield: 4 servings.

Nutrients Per Serving: Calories 141; Protein 10 g; Carbohydrates 17 g; Total Fat 5 g; Saturated Fat 1 g; Cholesterol 4 mg; Fiber 1 g; Sodium 755 mg

Creamy Leek and Cauliflower Soup

RECIPE

1 head cauliflower, chopped

2 tablespoons butter

4 large leeks, chopped

4 cups chicken or vegetable stock

pinch white pepper

1 (12-ounce) can evaporated skim milk

Combine cauliflower with enough water to cover in a saucepan. Bring to a boil; reduce heat. Cover and simmer for 2 minutes or until soft; drain. Heat butter in a large saucepan until melted. Add leeks and sauté until tender. Add cauliflower, stock and white pepper and mix well. Simmer, covered, for 30 minutes. Purée soup in batches in a blender until smooth. Return to the saucepan. Add milk and heat to serving temperature, stirring frequently. Ladle into soup bowls and top with seasoned croutons or chopped fresh chives. Yield: 4 servings.

Nutrients Per Serving: Calories 232; Protein 12 g; Carbohydrates 34 g; Total Fat 7 g; Saturated Fat 4 g; Cholesterol 20 mg; Fiber 6 g; Sodium 907 mg

Mushroom Barley Soup

4 (10-ounce) cans beef broth

2 1/2 cups water

3 large carrots, chopped

2 yellow onions, chopped

1 cup mushrooms, sliced

1 cup uncooked pearl barley

salt and pepper to taste

1/4 cup chopped fresh parsley

Combine beef broth and water in a large saucepan and bring to a boil. Reduce heat to a simmer. Add carrots, onions, mushrooms, barley, salt and pepper and cook for 30 minutes or until tender. Ladle into soup bowls and sprinkle with parsley.
Yield: 8 servings.

Nutrients Per Serving: Calories 138; Protein 7 g; Carbohydrates 25 g; Total Fat 2 g;
Saturated Fat <1 g; Cholesterol 1 mg; Fiber 5 g; Sodium 1104 mg

Old-Fashioned Cream of Mushroom Soup

1/4 cup (1/2 stick) butter

5 cups sliced mushrooms

1 cup finely chopped onion

1/3 cup finely chopped celery

1/4 cup flour

4 cups chicken broth

1 cup heavy cream

1/2 teaspoon salt

1/4 teaspoon pepper

1/4 cup dry sherry

2 tablespoons chopped fresh parsley

Heat butter in a large saucepan until melted. Add mushrooms, onion and celery and sauté until tender. Stir in flour and cook 2 minutes. Pour in chicken broth, reduce heat. Simmer, covered, for 30 minutes. Stir in cream, salt and pepper and simmer for 5 minutes. Remove from heat and stir in the sherry. Ladle into soup bowls and sprinkle with parsley. Yield: 6 servings.

Nutrients Per Serving: Calories 283; Protein 7 g; Carbohydrates 11 g; Total Fat 24 g; Saturated Fat 14 g; Cholesterol 75 mg; Fiber 1 g; Sodium 815 mg

Portobello Mushroom Soup

2 tablespoons olive or vegetable oil

1 1/2 cups thinly sliced onions, separated into rings

4 ounces Portobello or button mushrooms,

quartered and thinly sliced

5 cups water

3 beef bouillon cubes

1/2 teaspoon dried thyme

4 ounces orzo, uncooked

1 tablespoon dry sherry

salt and freshly ground pepper to taste

Heat olive oil in a large saucepan. Add onions and mushrooms and sauté until tender. Add water, bouillon cubes and thyme and mix well. Bring to a boil. Stir in orzo; reduce heat. Cook for 12 minutes or until orzo is tender, stirring frequently. Stir in sherry; cook 2 minutes longer. Add salt and pepper and mix well. Ladle into soup bowls and sprinkle with grated Parmesan cheese. Yield: 5 (1-cup) servings.

Impress company with an easy gourmet-style soup. On weeknights,
use button mushrooms and skip the sherry.

Nutrients Per Serving: Calories 159; Protein 4 g; Carbohydrates 21 g; Total Fat 6 g;
Saturated Fat 1 g; Cholesterol <1 mg; Fiber 1 g; Sodium 523 mg

French Onion Soup

2 teaspoons butter

2 red onions, thinly sliced

3 cups reduced-sodium chicken broth

1 cup reduced-sodium beef broth

1/4 cup dry red wine

2 large sprigs parsley

2 large sprigs thyme

3 tablespoons balsamic vinegar

freshly ground pepper to taste

1/2 French baguette, sliced 3/4 inch thick

1/2 cup (2 ounces) shredded low-fat Swiss cheese

2 tablespoons grated Asiago cheese

Coat a large saucepan with nonstick cooking spray. Add butter and melt over medium heat. Add onions and stir to coat. Cook for 15 minutes or until onions have browned, stirring occasionally. Reduce heat to medium-low and continue to cook, covered, for 30 minutes or until onions are a rich brown color, stirring frequently. Pour in chicken broth, beef broth and wine. Increase heat to high and bring to a boil. Tie sprigs of parsley and thyme together with kitchen twine and add to the soup. Reduce heat and simmer, partially covered, for 20 minutes. Discard parsley and thyme. Stir in vinegar and pepper. Ladle soup into ovenproof soup bowls and top each serving with 2 slices French baguette. Sprinkle with Swiss cheese and Asiago cheese. Broil or bake at 450 degrees until cheese has melted and begins to brown. Yield: 6 servings.

Nutrients Per Serving: Calories 97; Protein 6 g; Carbohydrates 8 g; Total Fat 4 g; Saturated Fat 2 g; Cholesterol 11 mg; Fiber 1 g; Sodium 130 mg

Swiss Cheese and Onion Soup

2 tablespoons olive oil

3 cups thinly sliced sweet onions

1 garlic clove, minced

1 teaspoon salt

3/4 teaspoon dry mustard

2 cups chicken stock

2 tablespoons butter

3 tablespoons flour

1/2 cup evaporated skim milk, warmed

1 1/2 cups (6 ounces) grated Swiss cheese

1 tablespoon dry sherry

1/2 teaspoon prepared horseradish

pepper to taste

1/2 teaspoon soy sauce

dash each of hot red pepper sauce and Worcestershire sauce

plain yogurt as needed

Heat olive oil in a large saucepan. Add onions, garlic, salt and dry mustard and sauté until tender. Pour in stock. Reduce heat to low and simmer for 15 to 20 minutes. Melt butter in another saucepan over medium-low heat. Whisk in flour and cook for one minute. Add milk and cook for 5 to 8 minutes or until thickened, stirring constantly. Stir in cheese, sherry and horseradish and cook until cheese has melted. Pour cheese mixture into onions and mix well. Add pepper, soy sauce, hot red pepper sauce and Worcestershire sauce. Cook for 8 to 10 minutes, stirring occasionally. Remove from heat. Stir in plain yogurt to make of desired consistency. Yield: 4 servings.

Nutrients Per Serving: Calories 355; Protein 16 g; Carbohydrates 18 g; Total Fat 24 g; Saturated Fat 12 g; Cholesterol 54 mg; Fiber 2 g; Sodium 1185 mg

Three-Bean and Ravioli Minestrone

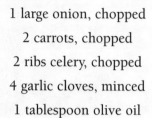

RECIPE

1 large onion, chopped

2 carrots, chopped

2 ribs celery, chopped

4 garlic cloves, minced

1 tablespoon olive oil

1 (10-ounce) package frozen baby lima beans

1 (15-ounce) can kidney beans, drained, rinsed

1 (15-ounce) can garbanzo beans, drained, rinsed

2 (14-ounce) cans diced tomatoes

3 (14-ounce) cans chicken broth

2 teaspoons Italian seasoning

1/2 teaspoon salt

1 teaspoon pepper

1 (7-ounce) package mini three-cheese ravioli,

cooked, drained

1 tablespoon chopped fresh parsley

Sauté onion, carrots, celery and garlic in olive oil in a large saucepan until tender. Add lima beans, kidney beans, garbanzo beans, undrained tomatoes, broth, Italian seasoning, salt and pepper and mix well. Bring to a boil. Reduce heat to medium and simmer for 20 minutes. Remove from heat and stir in ravioli and parsley. Yield: 6 (2-cup) servings.

Nutrients Per Serving: Calories 398; Protein 24 g; Carbohydrates 62 g; Total Fat 7 g;
Saturated Fat 1 g; Cholesterol 5 mg; Fiber 12 g; Sodium 2515 mg

Northern Italian Pasta Fagioli

1/2 cup finely chopped onion

1/4 cup finely chopped carrots

1/4 cup finely chopped celery

2 garlic cloves, minced

1 1/2 tablespoons butter

5 cups water

4 chicken bouillon cubes

1/4 teaspoon dried thyme

1/4 teaspoon crushed fresh rosemary leaves

8 ounces ditalini, uncooked

2 (19-ounce) cans cannellini or Great Northern beans

1/4 cup grated Parmesan cheese

2 slices lean bacon, diced, crisp-cooked

RECIPE 70

Sauté onion, carrots, celery and garlic in 1/2 tablespoon butter in a large saucepan until tender. Stir in water, bouillon cubes, thyme and rosemary. Bring to a boil; reduce heat to medium-high. Add pasta and cook 10 minutes or until tender, stirring occasionally. Drain and rinse 1 can of beans and mash with a fork in a bowl until smooth and creamy. Stir mashed beans and undrained can of beans into soup. Cook until heated through, stirring constantly. Remove from heat; stir in cheese, bacon and remaining 1 tablespoon butter. Yield: 6 servings.

Nutrients Per Serving: Calories 348; Protein 16 g; Carbohydrates 56 g; Total Fat 7 g; Saturated Fat 3 g; Cholesterol 13 mg; Fiber 8 g; Sodium 1276 mg

Southern Italian Pasta Fagioli

RECIPE 71

$^1/_2$ cup finely chopped onion

$^1/_2$ cup finely chopped carrots

$^1/_2$ cup finely chopped celery

2 garlic cloves, minced

1 tablespoon olive oil

4 cups water

4 beef bouillon cubes

1 (14-ounce) can diced tomatoes

1 teaspoon dried basil

$^1/_2$ teaspoon freshly ground pepper

8 ounces ditalini, uncooked

1 (15-ounce) can red kidney beans

Sauté onion, carrots, celery and garlic in olive oil in a large saucepan until tender. Stir in water, bouillon cubes, tomatoes, basil and pepper; bring to a boil. Add pasta; reduce heat to medium-high. Cook 10 minutes or until pasta is tender, stirring occasionally. Stir in undrained beans. Cook until heated through, stirring constantly. Ladle into soup bowls and drizzle with olive oil and sprinkle with grated Parmesan cheese. Yield: 6 servings.

Nutrients Per Serving: Calories 247; Protein 10 g; Carbohydrates 45 g; Total Fat 3 g; Saturated Fat <1 g; Cholesterol <1 mg; Fiber 5 g; Sodium 922 mg

Pasta Fagioli

1 onion, chopped

1 tablespoon canola oil

1¹/₂ cups (or more) water

1 (6-ounce) can tomato paste

1 tablespoon chopped fresh parsley

1 teaspoon dried basil

¹/₂ teaspoon salt

¹/₄ teaspoon crushed red pepper flakes

garlic salt to taste (optional)

4 ounces ditalini, uncooked

1 (15-ounce) can white beans

¹/₄ cup grated Romano cheese

72 RECIPE

Sauté onion in canola oil in a large saucepan until browned. Stir in water and tomato paste. Reduce heat to medium-low and simmer for 15 minutes. Stir in parsley, basil, salt, red pepper and garlic salt; simmer for 15 minutes. Meanwhile, cook pasta according to package directions. Add pasta and beans to sauce mixture and cook until heated through. Ladle into soup bowls and sprinkle with cheese. Yield: 4 servings.

Nutrients Per Serving: Calories 335; Protein 16 g; Carbohydrates 56 g; Total Fat 6 g; Saturated Fat 2 g; Cholesterol 7 mg; Fiber 8 g; Sodium 711 mg

Potato Leek Soup

2 leeks, sliced

4 medium red potatoes, chopped

2 tablespoons olive oil

3 (14-ounce) cans chicken broth

1/2 teaspoon dried thyme

1/2 cup buttermilk, sour cream or yogurt

salt and pepper to taste

2 tablespoons chopped fresh parsley

RECIPE 73

Sauté leeks and potatoes in olive oil in a large saucepan until tender. Add broth and thyme and simmer for 30 minutes, stirring occasionally. Process soup in a blender in batches until puréed. Return soup to the saucepan and cook over medium-low heat. Stir in buttermilk, salt and pepper. Cook until heated through, stirring frequently. Ladle into soup bowls and sprinkle with parsley. Yield: 6 servings.

This soup can be made ahead of time, frozen, and reheated. Add the buttermilk to soup in the saucepan or to each individual bowl just before serving. Red-skinned potatoes add texture and color, but you can peel them if you prefer.

Nutrients Per Serving: Calories 209; Protein 15 g; Carbohydrates 24 g; Total Fat 7 g; Saturated Fat 1 g; Cholesterol 3 mg; Fiber 3 g; Sodium 1566 mg

Cheddar Potato Soup

2 tablespoons butter or margarine

1/3 cup chopped onion

1/3 cup chopped celery

4 cups diced peeled potatoes

3 cups chicken broth

2 cups (8 ounces) shredded Cheddar cheese

2 cups milk

1/4 teaspoon pepper

dash paprika

RECIPE 74

Melt butter in a large saucepan. Add onion and celery and sauté until tender. Add potatoes and broth and mix well. Bring to a boil; reduce heat. Simmer, covered, for 10 to 15 minutes or until potatoes are tender. Purée soup in batches in a blender until smooth. Return to saucepan. Stir in cheese, milk, pepper and paprika. Cook over low heat until cheese is melted, stirring frequently. Ladle into soup bowls and top with seasoned croutons and chopped fresh parsley. Yield: 8 servings.

Nutrients Per Serving: Calories 254; Protein 13 g; Carbohydrates 18 g; Total Fat 15 g; Saturated Fat 9 g; Cholesterol 46 mg; Fiber 1 g; Sodium 535 mg

Sweet Potato Black-Eyed Pea Soup

1 medium onion, chopped

1/2 teaspoon minced garlic

2 teaspoons olive or vegetable oil

2 medium sweet potatoes, cut into 1/2-inch cubes

1/2 cup chopped green bell pepper

1 (15-ounce) can black-eyed peas, drained, rinsed

1 (14-ounce) can reduced-sodium chicken broth

1 (14-ounce) can diced tomatoes

2 ounces orzo, uncooked

1 tablespoon chopped fresh basil

1 teaspoon paprika

1/2 teaspoon salt

1/8 teaspoon freshly ground pepper

Sauté onion and garlic in olive oil in a large saucepan until tender. Add sweet potatoes, bell pepper, black-eyed peas, broth, tomatoes, orzo, basil, paprika, salt and pepper and mix well. Bring to a boil; reduce heat to low. Cook, covered, for 20 minutes. Yield: 10 servings.

Nutrients Per Serving: Calories 109; Protein 4 g; Carbohydrates 20 g; Total Fat 2 g; Saturated Fat <1 g; Cholesterol 1 mg; Fiber 3 g; Sodium 326 mg

Spinach Tofu Soup

1 (3- to 4-pound) chicken, cut up

1 onion, coarsely chopped

1 rib celery, coarsely chopped

1 carrot, coarsely chopped

salt and pepper to taste

8 quarts water

1 pound fresh spinach, washed, stemmed

1 pound firm tofu, cubed

white pepper to taste

Combine chicken, onion, celery, carrot, salt and pepper in a stockpot. Add water and bring to a boil. Partially cover and reduce heat to a slow simmer. Cook just until the meat falls from the bone, about 1 1/2 to 2 hours. Strain and return the stock to the stockpot. Reserve chicken for future use. Bring stock to a boil. Stir in spinach. Remove from heat and add tofu and white pepper; mix well. Yield: 4 servings.

Nutrients Per Serving: Calories 433; Protein 49 g; Carbohydrates 11 g; Total Fat 16 g; Saturated Fat 4 g; Cholesterol 144 mg; Fiber 2 g; Sodium 289 mg

Pumpkin Soup

1 pound pumpkin, peeled, seeded, cut into 1-inch cubes

1/2 cup each chopped celery and chopped onion

1 tablespoon olive oil

1/2 cup chopped peeled apple

1 cup chicken broth

1 tablespoon quick-cooking tapioca

2 cups low-fat milk

1 chicken bouillon cube

1 teaspoon sugar

1/2 teaspoon nutmeg

salt and pepper to taste

1/2 cup half-and-half or fat-free half-and-half

toasted pumpkin seeds to taste

Steam pumpkin until tender. Sauté celery and onions in olive oil in a skillet for 5 minutes. Add apple and sauté for 5 minutes longer or until tender. Combine celery, onion, apple and pumpkin in a blender or food processor and process until puréed; set aside. Bring chicken broth to a simmer in a small saucepan. Add tapioca and cook for 8 minutes; set aside. Combine puréed vegetables, milk and bouillon cube in a large saucepan and simmer. Add chicken broth, sugar, nutmeg, salt and pepper. Cook over medium-low heat until heated through, stirring frequently. Stir in half-and-half and cook about 1 minute or until heated through, stirring constantly. Ladle into bowls and sprinkle with pumpkin seeds. May substitute butternut squash for the pumpkin.
Yield: 6 (1-cup) servings.

Nutrients Per Serving: Calories 130; Protein 5 g; Carbohydrates 14 g; Total Fat 7 g; Saturated Fat 3 g; Cholesterol 14 mg; Fiber 1 g; Sodium 380 mg

Butternut Soup

1 leek, sliced

2 teaspoons olive oil

$^1/_2$ small butternut squash, peeled, seeded,

cut into 1-inch cubes

florets from $^1/_2$ head cauliflower

$3^1/_2$ cups chicken or vegetable broth

$^1/_4$ cup rolled oats

$^1/_4$ cup cooked couscous

salt to taste

chopped fresh dill weed or chives to taste

Sauté leek in olive oil in a saucepan until tender. Add squash, cauliflower, broth, oats, couscous and salt and mix well. Bring to a boil; reduce heat. Simmer, covered, for 30 minutes or until squash is soft, stirring occasionally. Process soup in a blender in batches until puréed. Return to saucepan and cook until heated through, stirring occasionally. Ladle into soup bowls. Sprinkle with dill weed or chives. Yield: 8 servings.

Butternut squash are softer than acorn or other types of squash
which make them easier to cut and prepare.

Nutrients Per Serving: Calories 72; Protein 4 g; Carbohydrates 10 g; Total Fat 2 g;
Saturated Fat <1 g; Cholesterol 0 mg; Fiber 2 g; Sodium 351 mg

Tomato Bisque

4 cups milk

1 onion slice

1/4 cup flour

1 (14-ounce) can whole tomatoes

2 teaspoons sugar

1/4 teaspoon baking soda

1/3 cup butter

1 teaspoon salt

1/8 teaspoon pepper

Combine milk and onion slice in the top of a double boiler set over simmering water. Cook until milk has scalded. Remove from heat; discard onion slice. Combine flour with a small amount of cold water in a bowl. Stir until there are no lumps and it is thin enough to pour, adding more water if necessary. Whisk flour mixture into milk. Cook for 20 minutes in double boiler, stirring frequently. Combine undrained tomatoes and sugar in a small saucepan. Simmer for 15 minutes over medium heat. Stir in baking soda. Remove from heat; drain, reserving the liquid. Finely chop tomatoes. Add tomatoes, reserved tomato liquid, butter, salt and pepper to milk mixture and cook until heated through, stirring occasionally. Yield: 6 servings.

Nutrients Per Serving: Calories 228; Protein 7 g; Carbohydrates 16 g; Total Fat 16 g; Saturated Fat 10 g; Cholesterol 50 mg; Fiber 1 g; Sodium 722 mg

Tomato Orzo Soup

1 (14-ounce) can whole tomatoes or

stewed tomatoes

6 cups water

1 (6-ounce) can tomato paste

2 beef bouillon cubes

1 tablespoon sugar

1 tablespoon dried minced onion

1 teaspoon dried basil

4 ounces orzo, uncooked

Drain and chop tomatoes, reserving liquid. Combine tomatoes, reserved liquid, water, tomato paste, bouillon cubes, sugar, onion and basil in a large saucepan and mix well. Bring to a boil. Stir in orzo; reduce heat to medium-high. Cook for 10 minutes or until orzo is tender, stirring frequently. Ladle into soup bowls and sprinkle with grated Parmesan cheese. Yield: 8 (1-cup) servings.

Nutrients Per Serving: Calories 89; Protein 3 g; Carbohydrates 19 g; Total Fat 1 g;
Saturated Fat <1 g; Cholesterol <1 mg; Fiber 2 g; Sodium 459 mg

Light Vegetable Stock

2 tablespoons vegetable oil

4 ribs celery, coarsely chopped

2 medium onions, coarsely chopped

1 cup coarsely chopped parsnip

1 cup coarsely chopped turnip

1/4 cup chopped mushroom stems

4 1/2 cups water

3 peppercorns

2 teaspoons salt

bouquet garni of thyme sprigs, parsley stems and bay leaf

Heat oil in a large stockpot. Add celery, onions, parsnip, turnip and mushrooms and sauté until tender. Add water, peppercorns, salt and bouquet garni. Bring to a boil, stirring occasionally. Reduce heat to low and simmer for 30 minutes. Strain, pressing on vegetables to extract as much juice as possible. Discard vegetables and seasonings. Let stock cool to room temperature. Cover with plastic wrap and refrigerate until ready to use. Yield: 5 cups.

Nutrients Per Serving: Calories 98; Protein 1 g; Carbohydrates 12 g; Total Fat 6 g;
Saturated Fat 1 g; Cholesterol 0 mg; Fiber 3 g; Sodium 980 mg

Easy and Tasty Vegetable Soup

3 or 4 beef or oxtail bones

1 gallon water

4 medium potatoes, peeled, diced

3 or 4 carrots, chopped

2 or 3 ribs celery, chopped

1 medium onion, chopped

1 (16-ounce) package frozen mixed vegetables

1 (14-ounce) can diced tomatoes

1 small bunch parsley, chopped

salt and pepper to taste

Combine bones and water in a saucepan. Simmer for 4 hours. Strain to remove all fat, reserving broth. Return reserved broth to saucepan. Add potatoes, carrots, celery and onion and cook over medium heat for 30 minutes or until vegetables are tender. Stir in frozen mixed vegetables, undrained tomatoes and parsley. Season with salt and pepper. Reduce heat to low. Simmer, covered, for 30 minutes or until vegetables are tender, stirring occasionally. For additional flavor, add 2 to 3 beef bouillon cubes with potatoes, carrots, celery and onion. Yield: 10 servings.

Nutrients Per Serving: Calories 125; Protein 4 g; Carbohydrates 28 g; Total Fat 1 g;
Saturated Fat <1 g; Cholesterol 0 mg; Fiber 5 g; Sodium 103 mg

Simple Vegetable Beef-Flavored Soup

1 (14-ounce) can reduced-sodium beef broth

1 (8-ounce) can no-salt added tomato sauce

1 cup water

1/2 cup baby carrots, sliced

1/2 cup minced celery

1 cup shredded cabbage

2 tablespoons dried minced onion

1/2 tablespoon dried parsley flakes

1/2 teaspoon minced garlic

6 drops of hot red pepper sauce

Combine broth, tomato sauce, water, carrots, celery, cabbage, onion, parsley, garlic and hot red pepper sauce in a saucepan and mix well. Bring to a boil; reduce heat. Simmer for 15 minutes or until carrots are tender, stirring occasionally. Yield: 4 servings.

Use vegetable broth instead of beef broth to make this soup vegetarian.

Add 1/2 cup green beans or broccoli florets for a heartier soup.

Nutrients Per Serving: Calories 54; Protein 3 g; Carbohydrates 9 g; Total Fat 1 g;
Saturated Fat <1 g; Cholesterol 0 mg; Fiber 2 g; Sodium 71 mg

Vegetable Noodle Soup

4 ounces egg noodles, uncooked

2 (14-ounce) cans vegetable or chicken broth

2 cups tomato juice

1 cup shredded cabbage

1 potato, peeled, cut into 1/2-inch cubes

1/2 cup sliced celery

1/2 cup sliced carrots

1/2 cup chopped onion

1/2 cup cut green beans

1/2 cup whole kernel corn

1/2 cup sweet peas

1 bay leaf

1 teaspoon dried thyme

1/2 cup sour cream

2 tablespoons chopped fresh parsley

Combine noodles, broth, tomato juice, cabbage, potato, celery, carrots, onion, beans, corn, peas, bay leaf and thyme in a large saucepan and mix well. Bring to a boil; reduce heat. Simmer, covered, for 30 minutes or until the vegetables are tender. Discard bay leaf. Ladle into soup bowls and top each serving with 1 tablespoon of sour cream and sprinkle with parsley. Yield: 8 (1-cup) servings.

Nutrients Per Serving: Calories 174; Protein 6 g; Carbohydrates 29 g; Total Fat 4 g; Saturated Fat 2 g; Cholesterol 20 mg; Fiber 4 g; Sodium 863 mg

Quick and Easy Vegetable Soup

2 (10-ounce) cans beef broth

2 cups water

1 (16-ounce) package frozen

mixed vegetables

1 (14-ounce) can stewed tomatoes

1/2 teaspoon salt

1/4 teaspoon pepper

RECIPE 85

Combine broth and water in a saucepan and bring to a boil. Stir in mixed vegetables, undrained tomatoes, salt and pepper. Reduce heat and simmer, covered, for 30 minutes or until vegetables are tender, stirring occasionally. Yield: 4 servings.

Since this is a basic soup recipe, you may add any vegetable or herb that you prefer. Some suggestions are shredded cabbage, chopped zucchini, diced turnips, fresh tomatoes, sliced okra, bay leaf, or parsley. For added nutrition, sprinkle with shredded low-fat cheese. This soup is also good topped with seasoned croutons.

Nutrients Per Serving: Calories 126; Protein 8 g; Carbohydrates 22 g; Total Fat 2 g;
Saturated Fat <1 g; Cholesterol 1 mg; Fiber 6 g; Sodium 1653 mg

Vichyssoise

1 cup sliced leeks

1 cup diced potato

2 cups chicken broth

$1/8$ teaspoon white pepper

salt to taste

$1/4$ cup whole milk

Combine leeks, potato, broth, white pepper and salt in a saucepan. Bring to a boil; reduce heat. Simmer, covered, for 40 minutes, stirring occasionally. Remove from heat; let cool in refrigerator for 15 minutes. Process soup 1 cup at a time in a blender until puréed. Stir in milk. Cover with plastic wrap and refrigerate until cold. Ladle into chilled soup bowls and sprinkle with minced fresh chives. Yield: 3 (8-ounce) servings.

Nutrients Per Serving: Calories 96; Protein 5 g; Carbohydrates 15 g; Total Fat 2 g;
Saturated Fat 1 g; Cholesterol 3 mg; Fiber 1 g; Sodium 536 mg

Cauliflower Vichyssoise with Chive Cream

Soup

5 cups water

florets from 1 head cauliflower

1/3 cup chives, cut 1/4 inch long

1/2 teaspoon coarse salt

2/3 cup half-and-half

salt and pepper to taste

Chive Cream

1/3 cup half-and-half

1/3 cup chives, cut 1/4 inch long

2 tablespoons water

pinch salt

For the soup, combine water, cauliflower, chives and salt in a saucepan and mix well. Bring to a boil; reduce heat. Simmer, covered, for 25 minutes or until cauliflower is tender. Purée in batches in a blender until smooth, gradually adding half-and-half. Transfer to a bowl. Season with salt and pepper and mix well. Chill, covered with plastic wrap, until cold.

For the chive cream, bring half-and-half, chives, water and salt to a boil in a small saucepan. Reduce heat and simmer for 1 minute. Purée in batches in a blender until smooth. Cover with plastic wrap and refrigerate until cold. Ladle soup into chilled bowls and drizzle with chive cream. Sprinkle with minced chives. Yield: 4 servings.

Nutrients Per Serving: Calories 105; Protein 4 g; Carbohydrates 8 g; Total Fat 7 g; Saturated Fat 4 g; Cholesterol 22 mg; Fiber 3 g; Sodium 345 mg

Zucchini Soup

2 tablespoons butter or margarine

2 onions, chopped

2 potatoes, peeled, diced

8 zucchini, chopped

$1/2$ teaspoon dried basil

$1/4$ teaspoon dried thyme

$1/4$ teaspoon dried rosemary

$1/4$ teaspoon white pepper

4 cups chicken broth

1 cup whole milk

$1/4$ cup instant potatoes

1 tablespoon soy sauce

$1/4$ cup chopped fresh dill weed

RECIPE

Melt butter in a large saucepan. Add onions and sauté until translucent. Add potatoes, zucchini, basil, thyme, rosemary and white pepper and cook for 5 minutes. Bring broth to a boil in a large saucepan. Stir in vegetables and herbs. Reduce heat and simmer for 15 minutes or until the potatoes are soft. Purée in batches in a blender until smooth. Return to the saucepan. Stir in milk and heat to a simmer. Add instant potatoes and soy sauce and mix well. Ladle into soup bowls and sprinkle with dill weed. Serve hot or cold. Yield: 8 servings.

Nutrients Per Serving: Calories 149; Protein 7 g; Carbohydrates 21 g; Total Fat 5 g; Saturated Fat 3 g; Cholesterol 12 mg; Fiber 4 g; Sodium 608 mg

Black Bean Soup

1 large onion, chopped

2 garlic cloves, minced

8 cups canned vegetable broth

2 cups canned black beans

2 carrots, cut into $^1/_2$-inch slices

$^1/_4$ cup orange juice

$1^1/_2$ teaspoons cumin

1 teaspoon chili powder

$^1/_4$ cup chopped fresh cilantro

$^1/_2$ cup nonfat sour cream

Coat a large saucepan with nonstick cooking spray. Add onion and garlic and sauté until tender. Add broth and black beans and bring to a boil. Stir in carrots, orange juice, cumin and chili powder. Reduce heat and simmer for 45 minutes. Pour soup into a blender, reserving 1 cup. Process until smooth. Return soup to the saucepan. Stir in the reserved 1 cup soup and 2 tablespoons of the cilantro. Ladle into soup bowls and top each serving with 2 tablespoons of sour cream and the remaining cilantro.
Yield: 4 servings.

Nutrients Per Serving: Calories 220; Protein 14 g; Carbohydrates 37 g; Total Fat 3 g; Saturated Fat <1 g; Cholesterol 0 mg; Fiber 9 g; Sodium 2441 mg

Black Bean Soup for a Crowd

1/2 cup vegetable oil

5 onions, finely chopped

4 tablespoons minced garlic

3 (28-ounce) cans whole tomatoes

11/3 cups water

4 teaspoons cumin

1 teaspoon cayenne pepper

8 (15-ounce) cans black beans

40 sun-dried tomatoes, chopped

1 cup chopped fresh cilantro

RECIPE 90

Heat oil in a large saucepan. Add onions and garlic and sauté until tender. Drain and chop tomatoes, reserving liquid. Add tomatoes, reserved liquid, water, cumin and cayenne pepper to the onions and garlic and mix well. Bring to a boil; reduce heat. Simmer for 5 minutes. Add undrained beans and sun-dried tomatoes and simmer for 10 to 15 minutes longer, stirring occasionally. Stir in cilantro. Process 1/2 of the bean mixture in a blender until puréed. Return the purée to saucepan and mix well. Add water or tomato juice if soup is too thick. Ladle into soup bowls and serve with a dollop of sour cream or plain yogurt. May be frozen for future use.

Makes 20 (6-ounce) servings.

Nutrients Per Serving: Calories 243; Protein 12 g; Carbohydrates 33 g; Total Fat 7 g; Saturated Fat 1 g; Cholesterol 0 mg; Fiber 12 g; Sodium 786 mg

Picante Black Bean Soup

RECIPE 91

4 slices bacon, diced

1 large onion, chopped

1 garlic clove, minced

2 (15-ounce) cans black beans

1 (14-ounce) can beef broth

1½ cups water

3/4 cup picante sauce or salsa

½ teaspoon dried oregano leaves

salt to taste

Fry bacon in a 3-quart saucepan until crisp; drain, reserving the drippings. Sauté onion and garlic in reserved drippings for 3 minutes. Add beans, broth, water, picante sauce, oregano and salt and mix well. Simmer, covered, for 20 minutes, stirring occasionally. Ladle into soup bowls and top with a dollop of sour cream and sprinkle with bacon. Yield: 8 (1-cup) servings.

Nutrients Per Serving: Calories 179; Protein 8 g; Carbohydrates 18 g; Total Fat 8 g; Saturated Fat 3 g; Cholesterol 8 mg; Fiber 6 g; Sodium 907 mg

Fast and Easy Black Bean Soup

3 (15-ounce) cans black beans,

drained, rinsed

2 cups water

1 cup salsa

Combine beans, water and salsa in a saucepan. Bring to a boil; reduce heat. Simmer over medium-low heat for 10 to 15 minutes, stirring occasionally. Purée soup in batches in a blender until smooth. Return to saucepan and heat to serving temperature, stirring frequently. Ladle into soup bowls and top with a dollop of reduced-fat sour cream and chopped green onions. Yield: 5 (1-cup) servings.

Unlike many soup recipes, this one is ready in a flash and contains only 3 ingredients. You can use dried black beans and fresh homemade salsa to reduce the sodium content, but then it wouldn't be fast and easy.

Nutrients Per Serving: Calories 216; Protein 13 g; Carbohydrates 34 g; Total Fat 2 g; Saturated Fat <1 g; Cholesterol 0 mg; Fiber 14 g; Sodium 958 mg

Old-Fashioned Black Bean Soup

2¹/₂ cups dried black beans

2 quarts chicken broth

2 quarts water

1 pound carrots, chopped

1 bunch celery, chopped

3 garlic cloves, mashed

2 large onions, chopped

1 small jalapeño chile, seeded, minced

6 to 8 peppercorns

1 bay leaf

grated zest of 1 lemon

juice of 1 lemon

salt and pepper to taste

Sort and rinse beans. Soak in water to cover overnight. Drain beans and place in a large stockpot. Add broth, water, carrots, celery, garlic, onions, jalapeño chile, peppercorns, bay leaf and lemon zest. Cover and bring to a boil; reduce heat. Simmer, uncovered, for 2¹/₂ to 3 hours or until beans are tender. Discard bay leaf. Purée soup in batches in a blender until smooth. Return to stockpot. Add lemon juice, salt and pepper and heat to serving temperature, stirring frequently. Ladle into soup bowls and serve with lemon slices, chopped cilantro and minced green onions. Yield: 10 servings.

For a more textured soup, purée only half the amount, leaving half as whole beans.

Nutrients Per Serving: Calories 238; Protein 16 g; Carbohydrates 41 g; Total Fat 2 g; Saturated Fat 1 g; Cholesterol 0 mg; Fiber 10 g; Sodium 682 mg

Pesto Soup

2^1/2 cups dried white beans

2 carrots, diced

2 leeks, diced

2 tomatoes, diced

2 zucchini, diced

1 potato, diced

^{1}/2 cup green beans, diced

1 teaspoon salt

^{1}/2 teaspoon freshly ground pepper

^{1}/4 teaspoon dried sage

2 quarts water

2 ounces vermicelli, uncooked, broken into thirds

^{1}/2 cup prepared pesto

Sort and rinse white beans. Combine white beans with enough water to cover by 3 inches in a bowl. Let stand for 8 to 10 hours; drain. Combine white beans, carrots, leeks, tomatoes, zucchini, potato, green beans, salt, pepper and sage in a slow cooker. Pour in water. Cook, covered, on High for 2 hours. Reduce heat to Low and cook, covered, for 8 hours. Add vermicelli. Cook, covered, on High for 30 minutes longer. Stir pesto into soup just before serving. Yield: 12 servings.

You can find prepared pesto in the refrigerated case of the grocery store next to the fresh pasta and sauces.

Nutrients Per Serving: Calories 232; Protein 12 g; Carbohydrates 39 g; Total Fat 4 g; Saturated Fat 1 g; Cholesterol 0 mg; Fiber 13 g; Sodium 297 mg

Tortellini Bean Soup

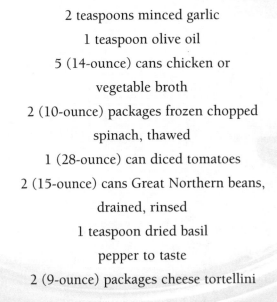

2 teaspoons minced garlic

1 teaspoon olive oil

5 (14-ounce) cans chicken or
vegetable broth

2 (10-ounce) packages frozen chopped
spinach, thawed

1 (28-ounce) can diced tomatoes

2 (15-ounce) cans Great Northern beans,
drained, rinsed

1 teaspoon dried basil

pepper to taste

2 (9-ounce) packages cheese tortellini

Sauté garlic in olive oil in a Dutch oven. Add broth, spinach, undrained tomatoes, beans, basil and pepper and mix well. Bring to a boil. Stir in tortellini and cook about 8 minutes or until tortellini is cooked. Ladle into soup bowls and sprinkle with Parmesan cheese. Yield: 12 (1^{1}/2 cup) servings.

This is a great soup for busy people since it only takes 15 minutes to make. It is also an excellent source of the anti-oxidants beta carotene and lutein.

Nutrients Per Serving: Calories 273; Protein 17 g; Carbohydrates 40 g; Total Fat 5 g;
Saturated Fat 2 g; Cholesterol 16 mg; Fiber 6 g; Sodium 769 mg

Dirt Soup
(Lentil Soup)

2 1/4 cups dried lentils

8 cups (or more) water

3 garlic cloves, minced

2 carrots, chopped

2 ribs celery, chopped

1 onion, chopped

1 cup tomato sauce

2 tablespoons olive oil

2 teaspoons sugar

salt and pepper to taste

Sort and rinse lentils. Combine lentils with enough water to cover in a 5-quart stockpot. Bring to a boil; drain. Return lentils to stockpot and add 8 cups water, garlic, carrots, celery, onion, tomato sauce, olive oil, sugar, salt and pepper. Simmer, covered, for 1 hour, stirring occasionally. Add additional water for a thinner consistency, if desired. Ladle into soup bowls; sprinkle with Romano cheese. You may serve over hot cooked rice. Yield: 8 servings.

Nutrients Per Serving: Calories 222; Protein 14 g; Carbohydrates 35 g; Total Fat 4 g;
Saturated Fat 1 g; Cholesterol 0 mg; Fiber 12 g; Sodium 203 mg

Hearty Lentil Soup with Winter Squash and Fennel

1 cup dried lentils

1/4 cup olive oil

1 onion, finely chopped

1 small fennel bulb

1 teaspoon fennel seeds

2 1/2 cups water

2 1/2 cups chicken broth

8 ounces butternut squash or pumpkin, peeled, diced

freshly ground pepper to taste

Sort and rinse lentils. Heat olive oil in a large stockpot. Add onion and sauté until tender. Dice fennel; reserve feathery tops. Add fennel to onions and sauté for 5 minutes longer. Add lentils, fennel seeds, water and broth. Bring to a boil; reduce heat. Simmer, partially covered, for 30 minutes, stirring occasionally. Add squash and cook for 20 minutes longer or until vegetables are tender. Finely chop fennel tops. Add to soup and cook 5 minutes. Season with pepper. Ladle into soup bowls and garnish with chopped fresh parsley. Add additional broth for a thinner consistency, if desired. Yield: 4 servings.

Nutrients Per Serving: Calories 350; Protein 17 g; Carbohydrates 40 g; Total Fat 15 g; Saturated Fat 2 g; Cholesterol 0 mg; Fiber 14 g; Sodium 841 mg

Split Pea Soup

3 quarts water

2 1/3 cups split peas

1 small ham shank

1 large onion, diced

2 tablespoons chicken soup base

1 bay leaf

1/2 teaspoon garlic powder

1/2 teaspoon oregano

1/4 teaspoon pepper

1 1/2 cups carrots shredded

1 cup celery, diced

Combine water, peas, ham shank, onion, soup base, bay leaf, garlic powder, oregano and pepper in a large saucepan. Simmer for 1 1/2 hours. Remove ham shank from soup and cut meat away from bone. Discard bone and add meat to soup. Stir in carrots and celery. Simmer 2 hours longer or until soup reaches desired thickness. Discard bay leaf. Yield: 8 servings.

Nutrients Per Serving: Calories 208; Protein 15 g; Carbohydrates 35 g; Total Fat 2 g; Saturated Fat 1 g; Cholesterol 7 mg; Fiber 13 g; Sodium 533 mg

Chilled Strawberry Soup

2 cups frozen strawberries

2 cups milk

1 cup heavy cream

1/2 cup sour cream

2 tablespoons white sugar or

to taste

Process strawberries, milk, heavy cream and sour cream in a blender or food processor until puréed. Stir in sugar. Cover with plastic wrap and chill 8 hours or overnight before serving. Yield: 6 servings.

Nutrients Per Serving: Calories 261; Protein 4 g; Carbohydrates 14 g; Total Fat 21g; Saturated Fat 13 g; Cholesterol 74 mg; Fiber 1 g; Sodium 66 mg

Cold Cantaloupe Soup

1 cantaloupe, peeled,
seeded, cubed
2 cups orange juice
1 tablespoon fresh lime juice
1/4 teaspoon cinnamon

Process cantaloupe and 1/2 cup of the orange juice in a blender or food processor until puréed. Stir in lime juice, cinnamon and remaining 11/2 cups orange juice. Cover with plastic wrap and chill before serving. Ladle into chilled soup bowls and garnish with sprigs of mint. Yield: 6 servings.

Nutrients Per Serving: Calories 71; Protein 1 g; Carbohydrates 17 g; Total Fat <1 g;
Saturated Fat <1 g; Cholesterol 0 mg; Fiber 1 g; Sodium 18 mg

Contributors

Tina Amato, MS, RD

Pam Aughe, RD

Irene Berman-Levine, PhD, RD

Mindy Bish, RD

Leisa Bock

Vanessa Briggs, MBA, RD

Cheryl Bruno Gamber, RD

Cindy Brylinsky, MS, RD

Martha T. Conklin, PhD, RD

Dagny Danga-Storm, RD, CDE

Corey DiLuciano, RD

Judy Dodd, MS, RD, FADA

Beth Egan, MEd, RD

Arlene Feleccia, RD, CDE

Denice Ferko-Adams, MPH, RD

Carol Folk, MS, RD

Jennifer Funaro, MS, RD

Joan Gangwer, MS, RD, CDE

Sue Gargano, MS, RD

Charlene Glispy, MS, RD, CFCS

Leslie Grant, RD, NHA

Theresa Gustafson, MS, RD, CDE

Norma Herr Harris, RD

Connie Holt, MS, RD

Jeanne Kandra, MS, RD

Kessey Kieselhorst, MPH, RD, CDE

Mary Klem, MS, RD, CNSD

Dottie Koteski, MS, RD

Patty Leyshock, MEd, RD

Jeanne Lillis, MS, RD

Cindy Linse, RD

Janice E. Mancini, RD

Juliet Mancino, MS, RD, CDE

Catherine A. McDivitt, RD, CSR

Ruth Anne McGinley, MS, RD

Ann K. McKenna, MS, RD

Catherine Meyers

Sharon Pascucci

Linda Pickwell, MS, RD

Janet Raytek, RD

Manette Richardson, RD, CDE

April Rudat, RD

Bette Saxton

Barbara Toth, MS, RD

Karen Virostek, MS, RD, FADA

Amy Virus, RD

Patricia Wenner, RD

Margie Wesdock, RD

Barbara Williams, RD

Common Measurements and Equivalents

3 teaspoons = 1 tablespoon

$1/2$ tablespoon = $1^{1/2}$ teaspoons

1 tablespoon = 3 teaspoons or $1/2$ fluid ounce

2 tablespoons = $1/8$ cup or 1 fluid ounce

4 tablespoons = $1/4$ cup or 2 fluid ounces

$5^{1/3}$ tablespoons = $1/3$ cup or 5 tablespoons + 1 teaspoon

8 tablespoons = $1/2$ cup or 4 fluid ounces

12 tablespoons = $3/4$ cup or 6 fluid ounces

16 tablespoons = 1 cup or 8 fluid ounces

2 cups = 1 pint or 16 fluid ounces

1 pint = 2 cups or 16 fluid ounces

1 quart = 2 pints or 4 cups or 32 fluid ounces

1 gallon = 4 quarts or 8 pints or 16 cups or 128 fluid ounces

Soup Glossary

BISQUE—A thick and smooth, rich cream soup, often made of puréed seafood.

BOUILLON—The French word for stock, it is the liquid drained off after cooking vegetables, meat, or fish in water with seasonings. It is used for sauce and soup bases.

BROTH—Enhanced stock in the ready-to-serve form.

CHOWDER—A thick, rich soup containing chunks of food (such as corn), but most often a seafood soup.

CONSOMMÉ—Stock that has been clarified so that it is crystal clear. It can be served hot or cold, and can be used as a soup or sauce base.

MINESTRONE—"Big soup" in Italian, a hearty vegetable soup that can serve as a complete meal. Generally includes pasta and sometimes peas or beans.

STEW—Dishes containing meat, vegetables, and a thick soup-like broth resulting from a slow simmer in a tightly covered pot.

STOCK—An intensely flavored broth that results from slowly simmering meat, fish, or vegetables in water. Stock is strained before use.

Soup Tips

- Soup makes a great medium for hiding leftovers like pasta, rice, vegetables, or meat.

- To reduce fat in homemade stock, pour into a shallow pan and place in the freezer until the fat floats to the top; it can be easily skimmed off.

- When making stock, cut vegetables to about the same size so that they all finish cooking at the same time.

- To determine how much soup to prepare, figure on 1-cup servings for a first course soup (3/4 cup if it is a cream soup) and 1^1/$_2$ cups for a main course soup.

- Cold soups, like gazpacho, should never be served ice cold because it dulls the flavor. Remove from the refrigerator at least 15 minutes before serving.

- To "wake up" flavor in a flat tasting soup, add a tablespoon of good wine vinegar or lemon juice. (For non-creamy soups only.)

- Garnish soups with complementary textures and colors. For creamy soups, use a crunchy garnish such as croutons. Swirl red pepper puree into corn chowder for a beautiful color contrast. Use leftover vegetables for great garnishes!

- Most soups freeze well for 1 to 2 months. Cream soups, soups with cheese, and soups containing rice or pasta are exceptions. Cream soups can curdle when reheated and soups containing pasta or rice absorb broth and change texture.

Index

Bacon
B.L.T. Pasta Soup, 20
Cauliflower Soup with Curried
  Onions, 19
Italian Bacon Cabbage Soup, 18
New England Clam Chowder, 54
Northern Italian Pasta Fagioli, 75
Picante Black Bean Soup, 96
Slow-Cooked Creamy Potato
  Soup, 21

Beans
Bean and Sausage Soup, 23
Black Bean Soup, 94
Black Bean Soup for a
  Crowd, 95
Fast and Easy Black Bean
  Soup, 97
Northern Italian Pasta Fagioli, 75
Old-Fashioned Black Bean
  Soup, 98
Pasta Fagioli, 77
Picante Black Bean Soup, 96
Southern Italian Pasta Fagioli, 76
Three-Bean and Ravioli
  Minestrone, 74
Tortellini Bean Soup, 100

Cabbage
Cabbage Soup, 48
Italian Bacon Cabbage Soup, 18
Reuben Soup, 25

Carrots
Carrot and Sweet Potato Soup, 64
Creamy Carrot Soup, 63

Cauliflower
Cauliflower Soup with Curried
  Onions, 19
Cauliflower Vichyssoise with
  Chive Cream, 92
Creamy Leek and Cauliflower
  Soup, 68

Cheese
Cheddar Potato Soup, 79
Last-Minute Cheddar Chicken and
  Noodles, 36
Swiss Cheese and Onion
  Soup, 73

Chicken
Chicken and Spinach Soup, 39
Chicken Corn Soup with
  Rivels, 41
Chicken Gumbo, 42
Chicken Noodle Soup, 35
Chicken Potpie, 40
Chicken Soup, 32
Easy Chicken Noodle Soup, 33
Hearty Chicken or Turkey
  Tortellini Soup, 37
Hearty Chicken Taco Soup, 44
Last-Minute Cheddar Chicken and
  Noodles, 36
Lemon Egg Soup, 38
Quick Chicken Noodle Soup, 34
Texas Tortilla Soup, 43
Wedding Soup, 15

Chili
Barley Turkey Chili, 45
Chili Meatball Supper, 11
Turkey Chili, 46
White Lightning Chili with
  Turkey, 47

Chowders
Corn Chowder, 65
Fish Chowder (A Real Maine
  Chowder), 58
Lobster Chowder, 57
Manhattan Clam Chowder, 53
New England Clam Chowder, 54
Seafood Chowder, 55
Seafood Corn Chowder, 56
Smoked Trout Chowder, 59

Cold Soups
Cauliflower Vichyssoise with
  Chive Cream, 92
Chilled Strawberry Soup, 104
Cold Cantaloupe Soup, 105
Gazpacho, 66
Vichyssoise, 91
Zucchini Soup, 93

Corn
Chicken Corn Soup with
  Rivels, 41
Corn Chowder, 65
Seafood Corn Chowder, 56

Fish
Fish Chowder (A Real Maine
  Chowder), 58
Seafood Chowder, 55
Smoked Trout Chowder, 59

Fruit
Chilled Strawberry Soup, 104
Cold Cantaloupe Soup, 105

Ground Beef
Cabbage Soup, 48
Chili Meatball Supper, 11
Easy Minestrone, 10
Hamburger Soup, 8
Italian Vegetable Soup with
  Beef, 14
Meatball Soup, 6
Meatball Stew en Casserole, 7
Quick Italian Beef and Vegetable
  Soup, 13
Taco Orzo Soup, 12
Wedding Soup, 15
What's for Dinner Hamburger
  Soup, 9

Ham
Creamy Ham and Potato
  Soup, 16
Philadelphia Pepper Pot
  Soup, 17
Split Pea Soup, 103

Leeks
Creamy Leek and Cauliflower
  Soup, 68
Potato Leek Soup, 78
Vichyssoise, 91

Lentils
Dirt Soup (Lentil Soup), 101
Hearty Lentil Soup with Winter
  Squash and Fennel, 102
Lentil Sausage Soup, 27

Mushrooms
Hot-and-Sour Soup, 67
Mushroom Barley Soup, 69
Old-Fashioned Cream of
  Mushroom Soup, 70
Portobello Mushroom Soup, 71

Onions
Cauliflower Soup with Curried
Onions, 19
French Onion Soup, 72
Swiss Cheese and Onion Soup, 73

Pasta
B.L.T. Pasta Soup, 20
Chicken Noodle Soup, 35
Easy Chicken Noodle Soup, 33
Easy Minestrone, 10
Hearty Chicken or Turkey
Tortellini Soup, 37
Italian Sausage Soup, 29
Italian Special Soup with Sausage, 30
Italian Vegetable Soup with Beef, 14
Last-Minute Cheddar Chicken and
Noodles, 36
Lentil Sausage Soup, 27
Northern Italian Pasta Fagioli, 75
Pasta Fagioli, 77
Pesto Soup, 99
Philadelphia-Style Minestrone, 22
Portobello Mushroom Soup, 71
Quick Chicken Noodle Soup, 34
Reuben Soup, 25
Skillet Goulash with Turkey, 49
Southern Italian Pasta Fagioli, 76
Sweet Potato Black-Eyed Pea
Soup, 80
Taco Orzo Soup, 12
Three-Bean and Ravioli
Minestrone, 74
Tomato Orzo Soup, 85
Tortellini Bean Soup, 100
Vegetable Noodle Soup, 89

Pork. *See also* Bacon; Ham; Sausage
Fish Chowder (A Real Maine
Chowder), 58
Philadelphia-Style Minestrone, 22

Potatoes
Cheddar Potato Soup, 79
Creamy Ham and Potato Soup, 16
Kielbasa Stew, 24
Portuguese Soup, 26
Potato Leek Soup, 78
Slow-Cooked Creamy Potato
Soup, 21
Vichyssoise, 91

Rice
Cabbage Soup, 48
Italian Bacon Cabbage Soup, 18
Philadelphia Pepper Pot Soup, 17

Sausage
Bean and Sausage Soup, 23
Clancy's Pub Soup, 28
Italian Sausage Soup, 29
Italian Special Soup with
Sausage, 30
Kielbasa Stew, 24
Lentil Sausage Soup, 27
Pepperoni Pizza Soup, 31
Portuguese Soup, 26
Reuben Soup, 25
White Lightning Chili with
Turkey, 47

Seafood. *See also* Fish
Callaloo (Crab and Greens
Soup), 51
Crab Tomato Soup, 50
Lobster Chowder, 57
Manhattan Clam Chowder, 53
New England Clam Chowder, 54
Seafood Chowder, 55
Seafood Corn Chowder, 56
Shrimp and Sweet Potato Soup, 52

Spinach
Chicken and Spinach Soup, 39
Italian Special Soup with
Sausage, 30
Spinach Tofu Soup, 81

Squash
Butternut Soup, 83
Hearty Lentil Soup with Winter
Squash and Fennel, 102

Sweet Potatoes
Carrot and Sweet Potato Soup, 64
Shrimp and Sweet Potato
Soup, 52
Sweet Potato Black-Eyed Pea
Soup, 80

Tofu
Hot-and-Sour Soup, 67
Spinach Tofu Soup, 81

Tomatoes
B.L.T. Pasta Soup, 20
Crab Tomato Soup, 50
Tomato Bisque, 84
Tomato Orzo Soup, 85

Turkey
Barley Turkey Chili, 45
Cabbage Soup, 48
Hearty Chicken or Turkey
Tortellini Soup, 37
Skillet Goulash with Turkey, 49
Turkey Chili, 46
White Lightning Chili with
Turkey, 47

Vegetables. *See also* Beans; Cabbage;
Carrots; Cauliflower; Corn;
Leeks; Lentils; Mushrooms;
Onions; Potatoes; Spinach;
Squash; Sweet Potatoes
Callaloo (Crab and Greens
Soup), 51
Chicken Gumbo, 42
Clancy's Pub Soup, 28
Cream of Asparagus Soup, 60
Creamed Beet Soup, 61
Creamy Broccoli Soup, 62
Easy and Tasty Vegetable Soup, 87
Easy Minestrone, 10
Gazpacho, 66
Italian Vegetable Soup with Beef, 14
Lentil Sausage Soup, 27
Light Vegetable Stock, 86
Pesto Soup, 99
Philadelphia Pepper Pot Soup, 17
Philadelphia-Style Minestrone, 22
Portuguese Soup, 26
Pumpkin Soup, 82
Quick and Easy Vegetable Soup, 90
Quick Italian Beef and Vegetable
Soup, 13
Simple Vegetable Beef-Flavored
Soup, 88
Southern Italian Pasta Fagioli, 76
Split Pea Soup, 103
Sweet Potato Black-Eyed Pea
Soup, 80
Texas Tortilla Soup, 43
Vegetable Noodle Soup, 89
Zucchini Soup, 93

Soup & Ladle Favorites

Pennsylvania Dietetic Association Foundation
P.O. Box 60870
Harrisburg, Pennsylvania 17106-0870
717-233-0558   •   717-233-2790 (fax)   •   www.eatrightpa.org

YOUR ORDER	QUANTITY	TOTAL
Soup & Ladle Favorites at $14.95 per book		$
Pennsylvania residents add 6% sales tax per book		$
Postage and handling at $3.50 per book		$
	TOTAL	$

Name _____

Address _____

City _____ State _____ Zip _____

Telephone _____

Payment: [ ] MasterCard   [ ] Discover   [ ] VISA
         [ ] Check payable to Pennsylvania Dietetic Association Foundation

Account Number _____ Expiration Date _____

Signature _____

Photocopies will be accepted.
For orders of six or more books, please contact the PADAF office for discount information.